TWAYNE'S WORLD AUTHORS SERIES
A Survey of the World's Literature

Sylvia E. Bowman, Indiana University

GENERAL EDITOR

CHINA

William Schultz, University of Arizona

EDITOR

Li Yü

TWAS 447

TWAYNE PUBLISHERS

E R R A T A

LI YU carries an incorrect series
number on the spine and half-title
page.

LI YU is TWAS 448

LI YÜ

By NATHAN K. MAO

Shippensburg State College

and

LIU TS'UN-YAN

The Australian National University

TWAYNE PUBLISHERS

A DIVISION OF G. K. HALL & CO., BOSTON

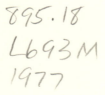
Library of Congress Cataloging in Publication Data

Mao, Nathan K
    Li Yü.

    (Twayne's world authors series ; TWAS 448 : China)
    Bibliography: p. 163–68.
    Includes index.
    1. Li, Yü, 1611–1608?—Criticism and interpretation. I. Liu,
Ts'un-yan, joint author. II. Title.
PL2698.L52Z75   895.1'8'4   76-56753
ISBN 0-8057-6283-3

Contents

About the Authors

Nathan K. Mao was educated at New Asia College, Hong Kong, at Yale and at Wisconsin and now teaches English at Shippensburg State College, Pa. His publications include translations of *The Twelve Towers* by Li Yü and *Cold Nights* by Pa Chin (with Liu Ts'un-yan). Both books were published by The Chinese University of Hong Kong.

Liu Ts'un-yan is Professor of Chinese at The Australian National University and has been a visiting professor at Columbia and Harvard. With a Ph.D. and a D. Litt from the University of London, he is also a Fellow of the Royal Asiatic Society and a Foundation Fellow of the Australian Academy of the Humanities. Among his many writings are *Buddhist and Taoist Influences on Chinese Novels, Chinese Popular Fiction in Two London Libraries, Wu Ch'eng-en: His Life and Career* and *Selected Papers from the Hall of Harmonious Wind.*

Preface

Dedicated to the art of living, Li Yü or Li Li-weng (1611–1680?) was a versatile writer of poetry, prose fiction, drama, and literary criticism. His life was colorful, his philosophy of life unusual, his fictional and dramatic works entertaining and innovative, and Chinese drama profited from his criticism and his dramatic theory. Yet in spite of his importance, we know of no full-length study of him in English. This, then, is an attempt to fill the gap.

We wish to thank Professor Robert Kalmey of Shippensburg State College for reading the manuscript and providing useful suggestions, and Miss Ludmilla Pasakaya of the Australian National University for translating from the Russian, for our reference, L. D. Pozdneeva's short but interesting piece about Li Yü. Our thanks also to Mr. Sanford Marlowe whose linguistic ability has made this a clearer and more readable book.

In preparing this book, Nathan K. Mao planned the general outline and wrote the first draft, while Liu Ts'un-yan was responsible for the historical and detailed data. However, the book is our joint responsibility.

NATHAN K. MAO
LIU TS'UN-YAN

Chambersburg and Canberra

Acknowledgments

Chapter 6 is reprinted in revised form from Nathan Mao, "Li Li-weng's Dramatic Theory," *Journal of the Chinese Language Teachers Association* 10, no. 3 (October, 1975), by permission of the Chinese Language Teachers Association.

Chronology

1611   Li Yü born in Hsia-chih District, Hupeh province.
1629   Father dies after the family returns to Chekiang.
1633   Probable date of publication of *Prayer Mat of Flesh (Jou p'u-t'uan)*.
1635   Trains under teacher Hsü Ch'ih; receives his first degree *(hsiu-ts'ai)*; lives at his retreat Yi-shan pieh-yeh, in Lan-ch'i, Chekiang.
1640   Abandons attempts to take the provincial examinations.
1642(?) Mother dies.
1644   Collapse of the Ming regime.
1645   Lives with Hsü Ch'en-chang (Hsi-ts'ai), subprefect of Chin-hua-fu, Chekiang; takes concubine Ts'ao; writes the play *Pitying the Fragrant Companion (Lien-hsiang-pan)*.
1647(?) Sells his retreat, Yi-shan pieh-yeh.
1648   Moves to Hangchow, Chekiang; takes the sobriquet "Fisherman of the Lake" *(Hu-shang Li-weng)*; publishes *A Collection of Early Poems (T'iao-ling chi)* either during the year or shortly thereafter.
1657   Moves to Nanking; journeys to Peking; builds Mustard Seed Garden on a hillock in Nanking; and probably publishes *Drama Without Sound (Wu-sheng hsi)*, a collection of short stories.
1658   Tu Chün writes preface to *Twelve Towers (Shih-erh lou)*; Li writes the drama *The Jade Hairpin (Yü sao-t'ou)*.
1660   Probably publishes *Twelve Towers*; three children are born to him between 1660 and 1662.
1661   His friend, Wang Tuan-shu, writes a preface to his play, *The Pair-eyed Fish (Pi-mu yü)*.
1663   Establishes friendship with Wang Shih-chen, Chou Liang-kung and others; publishes *A New Book on Government Administration (Tzu-chih hsin-shu)*, a collection of short essays by various authors on matters of government administration.
1665   Publishes *On the Ancients (Lun-ku)*, also known as *Li-weng pieh-chi* in 4 *chüan*, containing his comments on historical episodes and characters.

1666   Leaves for Peking; travels to Shansi and Shensi on a successful drama tour; acquires a favorite concubine, Ch'iao Fu-sheng.

1667   Issues a second collection of essays titled *A New Book on Government Administration;* stays for four months in Sian before going to Kansu.

1670   Spends some time in Fukien province before leaving for Kwangtung province.

1671   Publishes *A New Anthology of Parallel Prose (Hsin Ssu-liu ch'u-cheng);* probably also publishes *A Temporary Lodge for My Leisure Thoughts (Hsien-ch'ing ou-chi).*

1672   Leads his drama troupe sailing up the Yangtze River to Hupeh province.

1673   Publishes *Sayings of One School (Yi-chia yen)* and *Poetic Rhymes of Li-weng (Li-weng shih-yün);* concubine Ch'iao dies in Hanyang.

1675   Accompanies his two sons to Wuchow, Chekiang, where they sit for their first-degree examination.

1677   Moves back to Hangchow; purchases an old garden on a little hill in Hangchow and calls it Ts'eng-yüan.

1679   Writes prefaces to *Strange Happenings Old and New (Chin-ku ch'i-wen)* and *Painting Patterns of the Mustard Seed Garden (Chieh-tzu-yüan hua-chuan).*

1680(?) Li Yü dies in Hangchow.

CHAPTER 1

The Man and His Art of Living

I The Man

L I YÜ'S courtesy name was Li-weng, and some of his other names were Che-fan,[1] Li Tao-jen, Sui-an chu-jen, Hu-shang Li-weng, and Hsin-t'ing k'e-ch'iao. Although his ancestral home was the town of Lan-ch'i in Chekiang province, he was born in Hsia-chih, Hupeh.[2] His parents must have moved to Hupeh, probably for financial reasons, in or before 1611, the year of his birth. They were well-to-do at one time but had suffered financial reverses.[3] No definite evidence exists to show when the family moved back to Lan-ch'i from the middle Yangtze region. Internal evidence in his works indicates that his father died in 1629, that members of his family were stricken with an epidemic of some sort during the summer of 1630, and that his mother took care of the sick.

Li was known as a young genius, well versed in the classics and gifted in writing poetry, drama, and fiction. About 1635, at the age of twenty-four, he passed his first degree (*hsiu-ts'ai*) examination in Wuchow (Chin-hua). His essays on the classics were so good that they were printed and circulated by Hsü Ch'ih, the chief examiner. At that time or shortly thereafter he owned a retreat west of Lan-ch'i, known as Yi-shan pieh-yeh, and was a close friend of many local celebrities.

But his good fortune was soon threatened by political instability. Paralyzed by the misrule of powerful eunuchs, the Ming regime (1368–1644) faced the rebellion of Li Tzu-ch'eng in the western provinces and the ever-looming threat of the Manchus from the north. Turmoil and chaos reigned over much of the country. As early as 1639, in passing Tiger-claw Mountain, Li Yü had been robbed by bandits who spared his life. On another occasion, on his way to Hangchow for the provincial examination, he had to interrupt his trip and return home upon hearing reports of rampant civil disorder and bandit activities. He explained his feelings at the time as follows:

> Thinking anxiously of home I was.
> Heaven has set my date for return.
> *Poetry* and *Book of History* are met with death and confusion.
> I shall farm and fish, awaiting peace to come.
> The sail is broken, the wind is feeble,
> The boat is empty and hollow-sounding;
> Waves make noise.
> . . . .
> What is there to be done?[4]

Since scholars were expected to compete in examinations and, by being successful, to bring fame and honor to their ancestors, his poem conveys his sense of sorrow and regret at having to give up this last opportunity, after having failed in several previous attempts.

When Li reached thirty years of age (by Chinese reckoning, on New Year's Day, 1640), he commiserated with himself in a *tz'u* poem to the tune of "Courtyard Full of Fragrance" (*Man-t'ing fang*):

> Last night and today
> Only moments apart
> Yet they separate youth from old age.
> If one asks how old I am,
> I'm fully thirty years of age.
> Last night I was
> Nine and twenty, still boasting of adolescence.
> Alas, now I can't call myself old;
> I can't call myself young either.
> . . . .
> My wife too has added one year to her life.
> She prayed that I soon distinguish myself in examination halls.
> Awaiting my success, she forgot her birthday.
> Listening to my sighs and seeing me holding a cup in my hand,
> She counted with her tiny fingers, knitting her eyebrows together.
> Let's never talk about winning honors and rank; but let's
> Stay intoxicated.[5]

The year 1642 was marked by financial difficulties and probably the death of his mother.[6] In 1643 civil wars raged within China. Li

Tzu-ch'eng threatened Peking and captured it in 1644, proclaiming himself emperor of a new dynasty, the Shun. During this period of utter confusion, Li Yü had taken his family and fled to the country-side, as evidenced by the following excerpt from one of his poems:

> Cities and towns are dens for war horses;
> Allow me to live in the country.
> One wife and without too many children,
> Only one sack of books and my lute I shall take.
> Though the peach blossoms of Ch'in are distant,
> The flowing waters of Wu-lin smell sweet.
> Go I shall and now
> And never glance backward to the battlefield.[7]

Reflecting upon that three-year period of voluntary exile (1643–1645), Li wrote in *A Temporary Lodge for My Leisure Thoughts (Hsien-ch'ing ou-chi)*:

Between the collapse of the Ming regime and the victory of the Ch'ing, I desired neither academic success nor government position. I withdrew to the countryside and became fond of idling. In the summer I decided to receive no visitors but none came. I wore no kerchiefs, no clothes, and no shoes. As I lay naked among the lotus in the water, even my wife had difficulty in locating me. Sometimes I lay under the tall pines, unaware of the comings and goings of monkeys and cranes; other times I washed my inkstand under running brooks or brewed my tea using packed snow. When I yearned for melons, melons grew outside my house; when I desired fruits, fruits fell from trees. Those years were marked by extreme leisure, and the joys were the utmost in my life. . . . In reviewing my whole life, those three years were the most enjoyable.[8]

In the spring of 1645 he sought shelter in the house of Hsü Ch'en-chang, also known as Hsü Hsi-ts'ai, a mandarin in the prefecture of Chin-hua, Chekiang province. Hsü, a great admirer of Li's talents, welcomed Li and even provided him with a concubine named Ts'ao, a young widow formerly married to a Ming official. Though grateful to Hsü for his generous gift, Li was rather worried about how his own wife would react to his acquiring a concubine. To his surprise, his wife loved Ts'ao as much as he did, and the two women lived amiably together in the same bedroom.[9] Inspired by the harmonious relationship between wife and concubine, Li later composed the dramatic play, *Pitying the Fragrant Companion (Lien-hsiang-pan)*.

In 1646 the invading Manchus neared Chin-hua, and Li was forced to leave Hsü and return to Lan-ch'i. Accustomed to a good life, he was downhearted at losing Hsü's patronage. In a poem written on New Year's Eve in 1647 he wallowed in self-pity: "I write very little/ . . . My thin bones make me look like a crane/ and sparseness of hair makes me resemble a bald monk./ Every New Year's Eve brings an increase of sighs and sorrows."[10]

In 1647 Li sold his country retreat in Lan-ch'i and moved to Hangchow, the provincial capital of Chekiang province. Using a pseudonym, "Fisherman of the Lake *(Hu-shang Li-weng),*" he began writing in earnest. By 1655 he was able to support his family entirely through his literary endeavors, and his fame as a writer endeared him to many local celebrities. In Hangchow, where he stayed for approximately ten years, he wrote many poems and essays, as well as dramas and fictional works.

Li left Hangchow for Nanking in 1657, charging that his books had been pirated by unethical publishers in Hangchow and Soochow. Although this charge had some validity, other reasons might have been that he was in financial difficulties and that Chekiang's coastal cities were subjected to forays from Taiwan led by General Cheng Ch'eng-kung (1624–1662) (known to the West as Koxinga) who was a Ming official retaining his allegiance to the collapsed Ming regime. With the exception of periodic trips to other provinces, Li stayed in Nanking for approximately twenty years. Socially popular, he moved among fellow playwrights and other talented writers, artists, historians, and high government officials.

Among his friends was Chi Chen-yi (b. 1630), a young magistrate of Lan-ch'i. Originally from a very wealthy family in T'ai-hsing, Kiangsu, Chi was a well-known bibliophile, having collected many Sung and Yüan editions of classical works. His collection was probably the best north of the Yangtze. In his household, he kept three troupes of actresses for constant entertainment.

Then there was Yu T'ung (1618–1704), a historian and the author of a *tsa-chü* play, *Chanting "On Encountering Sorrow" (Tu Li-sao)*, and of other plays. He was most appreciative of Li's literary accomplishments, for Li had helped him revise some of his manuscripts. Besides Yu T'ung, there was Yü Huai (1616–1696), the author of several works on Chinese inkstones and on tea, and the compiler of the famous *Notes on a Wooden Bridge (P'an-ch'iao tsa-chih)*, a work of reminiscences of the lives of singing girls in Nanking. One of his essays entitled "On Shoes and Socks for Women" is included in Li's *A Temporary Lodge for My Leisure Thoughts*. Yü Huai also wrote critical commentaries on, or prefaces to, Li's works. Both Yu T'ung and Yü Huai enjoyed Li's dramatic productions. On one occasion, when Li Yü and his dramatic troupe performed in Soochow, they were so impressed by the productions that they wrote highly complimentary poems to mark the occasion. And when Li staged his revised play, "Brewing Tea," adapted from Lu Ts'ai's (1497–1537) *The Bright Pearl (Ming-chu chi)*, the performance did not end until daybreak; but it is reported that no one in the audience noticed how late it was as they had all been completely spellbound. In the audience were several small children, one of whom was Yü Huai's six-year-old son who was already quite familiar with the rhythm and able to follow the castanets beating time.

Among important officials, Li knew the three Hsü brothers very well. Hsü Ch'ien-hsüeh (1631–1694), Hsü Ping-yi (1633–1711) and Hsü Yüan-wen (1634–1691) had all distinguished themselves in the imperial examinations. Ch'ien-hsüeh and Ping-yi each won third place in the palace examinations in different years, and Yüan-wen won first place *(chuang-yüan)* in 1659. Another friend was the official, poet, and dramatist Wu Wei-yeh (1609–1672). Wu served both the Ming and the Ch'ing regimes but retired to T'ai-ts'ang in 1657 after suffering disappointments in his political career. Li visited him in T'ai-ts'ang several times. They compared notes on literature, feasted together, and Li wrote poems about Wu's villa and the beauty of Wu's flower garden.

Li also knew Wang Shih-chen (1634–1711), the author of the poem "Willows in Autumn," who advocated an intuitionist's view of poetry. Stationed in Yangchow between 1660 and 1665 and in Ch'ing-chiang p'u in 1669 and 1670, Wang admired Li's literary talent and presented him with some of his own publications. And with Chou Liang-kung (1612–1672), Li shared a common interest in compiling anthologies of both selected essays and letters by contemporaries. Chou served as grain intendant in Nanking from 1666 to 1669. Last but not least of Li's acquaintances was Ts'ao Hsi (d. 1684), the superintendent of the imperial textile factory in Nanking in 1663 and 1664, and the great-grandfather of Ts'ao Hsüeh-ch'in (d. 1763), the author of *Dream of the Red Chamber*.[11]

Personally, Li's Nanking period must also have been satisfying: his earlier fear of not being able to have male offspring proved incorrect. In 1660, at age fifty, his first son was born, and he gave a lavish celebration for his friends. Two more sons were born to him in the next two years. However, the new and welcome arrivals made him painfully aware of his increasing expenses. Shortly afterward he opened a bookstore, the Mustard Seed Garden, near his house. The Mustard Seed Garden was situated on what was called the Terrace of Marquis Hsiao, known to have been a former study of Chou Ch'u (240–299 A.D.), a scholar of the Three Kingdoms and Chin periods. The name "Mustard Seed" is a Buddhist allusion which implies philosophically that Mount Sumeru can be placed in a tiny mustard seed. It was a successful business venture, and its quality books are still prized by bibliophiles. Despite the handsome income derived from the Mustard Seed Garden, he was unable to meet his financial obligations. Returning from a business trip in the spring of 1666, just before Chinese New Year's Eve, he admitted that he had pawned all his valuables and could not even afford to buy the narcissus that he loved so much.[12]

Before long, Li journeyed to Peking, the national capital, which he had visited once before in 1658. By this time his financial situation seems to have improved, since he was accompanied by several servants and an unnamed concubine. En route, he tasted the apples, pears, and luscious grapes grown in the north, an experience fully recorded in some of his parallel prose. In Peking he was much impressed by the day-to-day life of its inhabitants, and made many friends including Kung Ting-tzu (Chih-lu, 1616–1673), the minister of justice and also a poet, and Songgotu (d. 1703), the influential Manchu nobleman who in 1689 signed the Treaty of Nerchinsk with the Russians.

However, the Peking air was cool and dry as well as dusty (since the wind deposited in the city the sand from the arid region north of the Great Wall), and this made Li uncomfortable and he wanted a daily bath. The Northerners, however, bathed only infrequently, and he had great trouble in obtaining a bathtub. When he finally succeeded, he declared that his happiness and intoxication were like having just made love to a woman.[13]

Li and his drama company moved on to Shensi via P'ing-yang, Shansi. In P'ing-yang, several local go-betweens approached Li urging him to buy a certain local girl as a companion to his concubine.

The girl, named Ch'iao Fu-sheng, was very pretty and clever. One day when Li's new play, *Female Phoenixes Courting the Male (Huang-ch'iu-feng)* was being performed with orchestral accompaniment, Ch'iao and another concubine were watching it and listening to the music behind a screen. When questioned by Li the next day about the background and some of the musical lines, Ch'iao interpreted them correctly. With the help of a local official, Li bought Ch'iao. Even though only twelve or thirteen years of age at the time, she soon learned to sing melodies in the Soochow pitch and became the leading actress in Li's troupe.[14]

Early in the following year (1667), Li and his company arrived in Sian, the provincial capital of Shensi, where they stayed for four months and probably gave public performances. Their host was Chia Han-fu, or Chia Chiao-hou (1606–1677), the governor of Shensi from 1662 to 1668. A vegetarian since birth, Chia was fond of compiling local gazetteers, and owned the famous "Garden of Half-an-Acre" in Peking where scholar-officials from Shensi were invited to stay during visits to the capital. Li had made suggestions to Chia as to how he could lend some individuality to the Garden's scenic spots. While in Shensi, Li led four members of his troupe to climb Mount Hua, which rises to twenty-two hundred meters and is one of China's five sacred mountains. In crossing its gorges, Li and his companions had to cling to strong ropes, and the girls had their shoes and shirts torn. Reaching the peak at last, they shouted and sang so loudly in their exultation that they "shocked the mountains."[15]

Toward the end of the year, Li and his company moved to Lanchow, Kansu, as guests of Liu Tou, the provincial governor. Then he was invited to visit General Chang Yung, also known as Fei-hsiung (1616–1684), who was posted at Kan-ch'üan to guard the northwest frontiers against the Mongols, the Eleuths, and the aborigines of Kokonor. On his way to Kan-ch'üan from Lanchow, Li noted that the aborigine girls let their hair grow to the ground and decorated it with pearls and jewels if they were rich, and with shells if poor, and that all the aborigines lived in tents made of horse or ox hides. When Li met the general, the latter urged Li not to bow because the general had been wounded so often that he could not reciprocate the courtesy.[16] Li thoroughly enjoyed the general's company and that of his other friends, some of whom had bought for him a few singing girls from Lanchow before his arrival.

One of the girls, Wang Tsai-lai, a year younger than Miss Ch'iao, had a very mild disposition and later played the male roles in Li's operas. Li loved both Ch'iao and Wang dearly. Ch'iao had been taught singing and acting in Sian by an experienced retired actor who had served in a prince's household in Lanchow at the time of the fall of the Ming dynasty. The new girls learned singing and acting from the talented Miss Ch'iao; with her as the principal teacher, Li's family troupe became a more viable organization, fulfilling one of his early dreams as stated in *A Temporary Lodge for My Leisure Thoughts:*

My temperament favors playwriting, and it is universally acknowledged that I have written many plays. Often putting myself in the actors' roles, I test the lines. I prefer to select my own actors. With my mouth I teach them the art of singing; with my body I demonstrate to them the required movements. Not only are my plays different from those written by other playwrights, but even the old songs composed by earlier playwrights become refreshingly original after I have deleted their flaws and given them a new style. [17]

His troupe performed regularly for friends and patrons. It inspired him to devote more time to playwriting and helped him formulate his dramatic theory, the scope and depth of which was unprecedented in the history of Chinese drama criticism.

In 1668 Li returned to Nanking. In 1670 he went to Fukien and Kwangtung provinces and returned again to Nanking the next year. He and his troupe had also been to the provinces of Shangtung, Honan, and Kiangsi, but these were short trips only briefly mentioned in his works and usually without dates. In 1672, in the first month of the lunar calendar, he and his troupe, under extremely adverse weather conditions, sailed up the Yangtze River to Hanyang, Hupeh. Their boat was battered by heavy winds and rain, and the trip from Nanking to Kiukiang took twenty-three days. At one time the waters were so rough and the wind so violent that many of the girls, huddled together in the cabin, broke into tears, fearing that the boat might capsize and they would be drowned. Fortunately, a favorable wind from Kiukiang helped them reach Hanyang in four days. There they disembarked. [18] In Hanyang and Wuchang, Li met many high officials who not only watched the performance of his plays but also presented handsome gifts to him, his concubines, and maids.[19] That winter, Miss Ch'iao gave birth to a daughter in Hanyang.

In the spring of 1673, Li traveled north by boat, probably only with a part of the troupe. Miss Ch'iao was by then already unwell, but she kept her condition secret lest she be prevented from accompanying him. Apparently the trip was short and the income from it meager, though the itinerary might have included Shansi or Peking. When they returned to Hanyang, Ch'iao's illness could no longer be concealed from Li and physicians were quickly summoned. She had been suffering from tuberculosis for over a year, and the physicians decided that she had malaria too, and concluded that the intense summer heat might have been the cause of her recent illness. Due to the lack of proper treatment, she died that autumn. A most capable assistant in Li's drama productions, she had also been very close to him personally and her early death was a crushing blow. He escorted her coffin back to Nanking and wrote more than twenty elegiac poems, bitterly lamenting his incalculable loss.[20]

Earlier, in late 1673, the little girl born to Miss Ch'iao also died. In a pathetic deathbed scene, the dying mother had entrusted the child to Miss Wang Tsai-lai's care, but Miss Wang was also ill and at the same time, very unhappy, since she was vying with another concubine for Li's affections.

In 1674 Li visited Peking for the fourth and last time, accompanied by two concubines, Miss Wang and a Miss Huang, both bosom friends of the deceased Ch'iao. Huang was pregnant, and Wang, while on the boat, had certain symptoms usually connected with pregnancy. Overjoyed at the prospect, she used her private savings to prepare baby clothes, but to her utter disappointment found, a month or so after her arrival in Peking, that she was not pregnant at all. She died shortly thereafter in Peking at the age of eighteen; Miss Huang gave birth to a son on the return journey with Li the following spring.[21] Like her friend Ch'iao Fu-sheng, Wang had had an excellent voice and was well qualified to play the male roles in Li's many plays. Her death, coupled with Ch'iao's earlier demise, drove Li to distraction. In addition to composing ten elegiac poems in Miss Wang's memory and a biographical account of his two beloved concubine-actresses, Li seemed to have lost all interest in life.[22] Moreover, his staunch patron, Minister Kung Ting-tzu, died in October, 1673, and Li's other Peking friends could not offer him much financial assistance. This was another sharp disappointment.

Whenever Li was away from Nanking with his troupe, his household's management was left to his eldest daughter, Li Shu-chao, who was married to Shen Hsin-yu, a distinguished painter. Li's second daughter Shu-hui was married to Yü Tzu-ch'en, of whom we know little. We do know that both daughters were well versed in the composition of *tz'u* poems, and from Li's *Complete Works* we know that he accompanied his two sons, Chiang-shu and Chiang-k'ai, to sit for their first-degree examinations in Wuchow in 1675. As old age and declining fortunes mercilessly haunted him, he yearned to settle permanently in Hangchow. Helped by a few friends, he purchased a home, Ts'eng-yüan, an old garden on a little hill in Hangchow. But he could move from Nanking to Hangchow in the spring of 1677 only after he had sold his house in Nanking, his woodblocks, his personal effects, and his jewelry to satisfy his debtors. After he had settled down in his new house, he fell from the second floor to the ground in an accident that almost took his life. Nonetheless, the same summer he again accompanied his two sons to take their examinations. After he returned, he had both malaria and dysentery. In 1678 his financial condition improved, enabling him to finish the construction of a few uncompleted houses on his property. In 1679 he wrote the preface to the first series of the *Painting Patterns of the Mustard Seed Garden (Chieh-tzu-yüan hua-chuan)*, collected by his son-in-law, Shen Hsin-yu and illustrated by another painter, Wang Kai. Shortly afterward, Li's health rapidly deteriorated and he died, probably in 1680.

To sum up, Li lived in Hsia-chih and Lan-ch'i until he was thirty-seven; he then moved to Hangchow and later to Nanking. During his Nanking years he made many trips to other provinces and visited Peking on at least four occasions. He died in Hangchow.

A writer, editor, publisher, and producer of dramatic plays without inherited wealth or government position, Li lived far beyond his means. His houses in Lan-ch'i, Nanking, and Hangchow were decorated with taste and elegance; his clothes and those of his family were of good and fashionable material; his board was always available to friends; his women were young and beautiful. On the other hand, the income from selling his own books and the profits from his bookstore were scarcely enough to meet the expenses of a household of more than forty members, which included his five sons, three daughters, a wife, concubines, maids, and other servants. His major source of income, it would seem, came from his drama tours.

For instance, during one of his trips to Sian, Shensi province, he was given enough money to pay off his earlier debts;[23] and on another trip an admiring patron gave him a concubine, Miss Ch'iao.

Despite the income from his tours, he was always strapped for money. Out of necessity he begged unashamedly from his patrons. Whenever rebuffed he complained bitterly about the shabby treatment given to professional writers by an unappreciative society. The following is an example of his frequent outbursts:

I have always considered myself a writer ever since I began to write. Though I dare not boast of the writing of grandiose prose, I am somewhat skilled in writing poetry, drama, and fiction. Without copying others, in the last several decades I, the Fisherman of the Lake, have entertained many. . . . But now I am hungry and without food, cold and without clothing. . . . Even peasants and hawkers can find enough to feed themselves. In olden days, even people with minor skills were treated with respect by the wise and the powerful. Examples are too numerous. And today many who have such petty skills as chess-playing, song-singing, ball-kicking, and storytelling are richly rewarded by officials who scheme to get their attention. On the other hand, I am too well educated. I shall not mention my many books, but the little one, *A Temporary Lodge for My Leisure Thoughts*, is itself unique. Now all my skills have been exhausted. I am without a load of rice, something with which to start the family stove, or money for daily expenses. I must borrow from another who may possess one single saleable skill. This is a shame for a man of my talents. True, there have been talents in the past that were not recognized but rather scorned by society, but they were either crafty, slanderous, or greedy. . . . Has anyone ever known me to be like that? Although an affable and contented man, I am about to starve to death. I do not seek pity from others and no one is offering any. This is my shame. . . .[24]

Strangely, no matter how serious his financial problems, he never seemed to consider reducing his expenses and offered the following excuse:

Relatives and friends have despised me for not accepting the difficulties of the time, for spending money too freely, and for my poverty today. But they do not understand that my past extravagances were not paid for by me but by others. Whatever food, provisions, and clothing I have were given to me. My few concubines were not purchased with my money but were given to me as presents. Many of them are dead now. . . . Die they may, but I can never sell them.[25]

Unwilling to compromise his living standards, he sacrificed his pride and begged from his patrons, fully aware of how difficult it was to please them, as he lamented in the following poem:

> The way of the world is not like that of old.
> Difficulties abound in journeying from one
>   place to another.
> That I not be as prosperous as others is the
>   will of Heaven.
> Friends forgive me for not desiring official
>   rank.
> My repeated silences. Dare I ever hope for much
>   from anyone?
> Ten thousand tribulations to bring a little
>   pleasure to my patrons,
> Hard work and diligent writing have given me
>   a meager living.
> How dare I dream of a precarious life in Hantan?[26]

II His Art of Living

The meaning of human existence has been the focal point of philosophical inquiry since Plato and Aristotle. The subject has also been examined and reexamined in China—by Confucius, Lao Tzu, Mo Tzu, and others. In examining Li Yü's writings, the reader is likely to discover that his view of life bears closer comparison to the classic Cyrenaic, Epicurean, and Utilitarian philosophies than to Confucian humanism, to Lao Tzu's renunciation of life and society, or to Mo Tzu's regard for the welfare of men.

Well aware of the viccissitudes of life—its illnesses, its countless hardships, and the ups and downs of personal fortunes—Li comments that life is so brief that every person must live it to the fullest within the limitations set by the Creator.[27] Taking essentially a biological view of life, he details in A Temporary Lodge the pleasures he takes in the clothes he wears, the food he eats, the places in which he lives, his daily activities, his inventions of little domestic items, the securing of happiness for rich and poor, his appreciation of nature, his methods of minimizing worries, the grooming of women, and the regulation of sexual needs.

Li says that a person should dress with discriminating taste. This principle is particularly valid when applied to women's clothing:

The important thing about women's dress is not fineness of material but neatness, not gorgeous beauty but elegance, not that it agrees with her family standing but that it agrees with her face. . . . If you take a dress and let several women try it on in succession, you will see that it agrees with some and not with others, because the complexion must harmonize with the dress. If a wealthy lady's face does not agree with rich patterns but agrees with simple colors, and she should insist on having rich patterns, would not her dress be the enemy of her face? . . . Generally, one whose complexion is white and soft and whose figure is light and round will be shown to advantage in any dress. Light colors will show her whiteness but deep colors will still better show her whiteness. Dresses of fine material will show her delicacy, but dresses of coarse material will still better show her delicacy. . . . But how few women are of this type! The average woman must choose her dress, and must not take any kind of material. . . .[28]

Humorously, Li comments that the mouth and the stomach are the two most unnecessary organs in the human body, but that man is afflicted with them and labors with all his energy to satisfy their needs: "I have considered this matter [of having a stomach] over and over again, and cannot help blaming the Creator for it. I know, of course, that He must have repented of His mistake also, but simply feels that nothing can be done about it now, since the design or pattern is already fixed. . . . "[29]

Discussing various vegetable and meat dishes, he observes that bamboo shoots make a superior dish if cooked with special care; he stresses the proper methods of preparing *fan* ("cooked rice"), porridge, and soup; and he places meat dishes last in importance, arguing that the fat contained in meat weakens a person's intellect. Comparing vegetarian versus meat-eating animals, he comes to the conclusion that the former are more intelligent than the latter. For instance, he sees meat-eating tigers as the dumbest of animals:

Tigers are the most stupid among the animals. How do we know? Because from books we learn that they will not eat small children. Why? It is not because they are not attracted to them; it is because they think that children are brave, since children show no fear of them. Furthermore, tigers will not eat drunken people. Why? Because they view the inebriants as fierce opponents when they are merely behaving irrationally.[30]

His comments on nonvegetarian dishes include extensive discussions of pork, lamb, beef, poultry products, and sea food, and he confesses a particular weakness for crabs:

There is nothing in food and drink whose flavor I cannot describe with the utmost understanding and imagination. But as for crabs, my heart likes them, my mouth relishes them, and I can never forget them for a year and a day, but find it impossible to describe in words why I like them, relish them, and can never forget them. Ah, this thing has indeed become for me a weakness in food, and is in itself a strange phenomenon of the universe. All my days I have been extremely fond of it. Every year before the crab season comes, I set aside some money for the purpose, and because my family says that "crab is my life," I call this money "my life ransom." From the day it appears on the market to the end of the season, I have never missed it for a night. . . . I used to have a maid quite devoted to attending to the care and preparation of crabs and I called her "my crab maid." Now she is gone. Oh crab! My life shall begin and end with thee![31]

In another passage he explains that he prefers crab because it meets the three requisites of food—color, fragrance, and flavor.[32]

For wine parties, he declares that he has five dislikes and five likes. While detesting excessive drinking, eating, all-night parties, wine-drinking games, and the cursing of fellow guests by pretended drunkards, he enjoys good companionship, delightful conversations, moonlight parties, the embarrassed looks on the faces of those who have lost in wine-drinking games, and the frank and candid remarks made by those "under the influence."[33]

Moving from culinary delights and parties to housing, he announces that notwithstanding his poverty and his years of wandering from one place to another, deprivation has not cost him his decorative expertise. His retreat, Yi-shan pieh-yeh, located at the foot of the Yi mountain in Lan-ch'i, featured bridges, pavillions, winding paths, fish ponds, running brooks, fruit trees, and green pastures. His house in Nanking, the famed Mustard Seed Garden, so named because of its small size, was decorated with taste and every room given a poetic name. And his last house, Ts'eng-yüan, was located on a hillock in Hangchow from which he had an unobstructed view of the West Lake.[34] He feels life has given him two special skills: training in music and a knowledge of architecture and interior house designs.[35] He says:

A man cannot live without a house as his body cannot go about without clothing. And as it is true of clothing that it should be cool in summer and warm in winter, the same thing is true of a house. It is all very imposing to live in a hall twenty or thirty feet high with beams several feet across, but such a house is suitable for summer and not for winter. The reason why one shivers when he enters an official's mansion is because of its space. It is like one person wearing a fur coat while the other does not even have a quilted jacket. On the other hand, a poor man's house with low walls and barely enough space to put one's knees in, while having the virtue of frugality, is suitable for the owner but not suitable for entertaining guests. That is why we feel cramped and depressed without any reason when we enter a poor scholar's hut. . . . I hope that the dwellings of officials will not be too high and big. For a house and the people living in it must harmonize as in a picture. Painters of landscape have a formula saying: "ten-feet mountains and one-foot trees; one-inch horses and bean-sized human beings." It would be inappropriate to draw trees of two or three feet on a hill of ten feet, or to draw a human being the size of a grain of rice or millet riding on a horse an inch tall. It would be all right for officials to live in halls twenty or thirty feet high, if their bodies were nine or ten feet. Otherwise, the taller the building, the shorter the man appears, and the wider the space, the thinner the man seems. Would it not be much better to make his house a little smaller and his body a little stouter? . . .[36]

Thoughtfully he suggests that simplicity, novelty, elegance, and refinement rather than luxury, elaborate decoration, and splendor should be emphasized in architecture.[37] An ideal house should face south, have a side door for emergency exit purposes, be situated on high ground, and be built with good weatherproof eaves.[38]

As one of the comforts of daily living, he invented the "landscape window" which looked out on the hills. The idea came to him quite unexpectedly. Sitting in his studio one day, he saw through the window a hill about ten feet high and seven feet wide behind his house "decorated with a miniature scenery of red cliffs and blue water, thick forests and tall bamboos, singing birds and falling cataracts, thatched huts and wooden bridges," representative of all the scenes usually found in a mountain village. To complete the picture he made a clay figure of himself as a fisherman holding a fishing pole in one hand and fixed it in a sitting position on top of a rock. Engrossed in the view, he was unwilling to close the window. Suddenly it occurred to him that the hill could be made into a "painting," and the "painting" into a "window." He instructed his boy-servant to "cut out several pieces of paper and paste them above and below the window and at the sides, to serve as the mounting for a real picture." When the "mounting" was completed, the space usually occupied by the painting was filled by the hill behind his house. Thus his window became a "living painting," featuring the hill and changing with the seasons.[39]

In addition to the "landscape window" he also devised a "fan-shaped window" to use on pleasure boats. With the "fan-shaped window" as a frame on a boat, the passengers would have a view of "the light of the lake and the color of the hills, the temples, the monks, clouds, haze, bamboos, trees on the banks, as well as wood-cutters, shepherd boys, drunken old men, and promenading ladies." Moreover, when the boat was either moving or at anchor, the scenery changed with the moving of the wind or the rippling of the water. On the other hand, the spectators on the banks could view the people on board drinking wine or tea or glimpse calligraphy if such was painted on the "fan-shaped window."[40]

To help other mortals attain maximum comfort and convenience, he improved such domestic items as screens, lamps, tables, curios, and cabinets. More specifically, he devised a heated armchair for winter and a porcelain cooling bench for summer. Recognizing that man spends one third to one half of his time in bed, he suggested that one build a narrow wooden shelf on which to place flower pots and affix it to the embroidered curtain which is part of the traditional Chinese bed. The thin wooden shelf should be wrapped in embroidered silk in such a way as to make it resemble odd-shaped stones or floating clouds. By so doing, Li exclaims: "My body is no longer a body, but a butterfly flitting about and sleeping and eating among flowers, and the man is no longer a man but a fairy, walking about and lying in a paradise."[41]

Although proper household conveniences give man a sense of well-being, he must learn to extract real joy from his daily activities, an art much neglected by the people. Li mentions the pleasure of washing up, dressing, eating, sitting, walking, or sleeping, and even the joys of going about naked and barefoot or going to the toilet. To him, a poor man using his legs was better off than a rich man traveling in a horse and carriage. In direct contrast to Confucius, who advised man to sit straight and erect, Li says: "Do not sit erect and look severe as if you were chained or glued to the chair. Hug your knees and sing, or sit chin in hand, without honoring it with the phrase of 'losing yourself in thought.' " If a person insists on sitting stiffly with head high and chest out, Li says: "He is sitting for his memorial portrait." As for standing up straight, Li suggests an alternative: "Stand straight, but do not do it for long. Otherwise, all leg muscles will become stiff and circulation will be blocked up. Lean on something!—on an old pine or a quaint rock, or on a bal-

cony or on a bamboo cane. It makes one look like one is in a painting. But do not lean on a lady! The foundation is not so solid and the
roof may come down!"[42]

To further enrich a person's life, Li recommends cultivating such
hobbies as playing chess or musical instruments; appreciating nature by listening to birds singing; raising domestic birds such as the
thrush or growing domestic plants; and engaging in good conversation with men of learning.[43]

Moving on from physical activities and the cultivation of hobbies,
Li discusses the art of securing happiness by different social classes:
(1) men of rank; (2) the rich; and (3) the poor. For the first, happiness
lies in helping their subjects achieve their aspirations. For the second group, securing happiness is more elusive:

> To teach a rich man to enjoy life would mean to ask him to give money
> away, which is difficult, to say the least. Having money, one thinks of
> managing it to let it grow and have more. Once he starts to manage money,
> there are endless worries and all peace of mind is gone. Also, one begins to
> worry about theft or robbery, or even being stabbed into the bargain. The
> worries arising from such fears of theft and robbery are equally demeaning.
> Furthermore, wealth makes one a target for envy, and one feels no one
> really cares for him. What chance is there for enjoying life? Such indeed are
> the penalties of great wealth. Should one therefore conclude that it is
> impossible to be happy though wealthy? I think not. One cannot be ex-
> pected to give a great deal of money away, but one can at least refrain from
> being grasping. . . . When one hears the tributes of the poor people, it is as
> good as having two orchestras, and when one receives honors or awards
> from the government, one's name goes down to posterity. Thus one obtains
> both honor and happiness. As to amusements, music, women, nice villas,
> pleasure parties, these things are easily available to the wealthy people as
> they are not to the poor. So what seemed to be difficult to attain can now be
> readily achieved.[44]

Regarding the poor, Li philosophizes:

> The art of being happy though poor consists in one phrase, think "it could
> be worse." I am poor and humble, but there are people poorer and more
> humble than myself. I have a big family to support, but there are people
> living alone and without children, and widows and orphans. I have to work
> hard on a farm, but there are people without a farm, or who would rather
> work hard on their farm but cannot because they are sitting in jail. It is a
> way of thinking, or of looking at it. The same situation may look like hell to

one and like paradise to another. On the other hand, always to want to compare oneself to one's better will breed a state of mind conducive only to one's own misery.[45]

Regardless of a person's importance or wealth, his happiness begins at home. Family happiness consists in one's being able to honor his parents while they are living, to love his brothers and sisters, and to cherish his wife. When one travels abroad, happiness comes from absorbing all the scenic sights, from getting to know the people of different regions, and from tasting that which one has never tasted before. In the spring, one should not indulge in excessive sexual activities but spend more time with nature and listen to the birds while visiting scenic areas. When summer comes, be mentally alert and physically prepared for the many illnesses that accompany hot weather. The fall, with its matchless splendor, is the time to invite friends on country outings. And in the winter, though the outside world be covered with snow and the house itself cold and dreary, one can still be happy by pretending to be a man traveling under adverse weather conditions. Thus, everything inside the house will seem to be warm and comforting.[46]

Finally, Li writes at length on women, prefacing his remarks with a confessional apology:

I am a poor man, and I have been cursed with all manner of ill fortune in my life. Not only have I never been close to exquisite, beautiful women, I have not even seen many ordinary looking women. How then dare I speak on the subject of feminine charm and beauty? I will only succeed in drawing ridicule from connoisseurs. Yet, even though I lack experience and expertise in the field, my interest in it has always been strong.[47]

Mirroring the views of seventeenth-century China, Li believes the grooming of women to be important, and he writes about such subjects as "Natural Manners," "Makeup," "Costume and Accessories," and "Cultivation of Talents" in his A Temporary Lodge. Under "Natural Manners," he discusses the fairness of complexion, the width of eyebrows, the size of hands and feet, and the brightness of eyes. More specifically, he feels that "the ten fingers and two hands of a woman are a definite key to her intelligence and her future fortunes. . . . If her hands are soft and her fingers long and shapely, she is likely to be intelligent. . . ."[48] Even though he likes tiny feet on women, he does not want them to be so small that they

are a burden to their owner.[49] Under "Makeup" he expounds on the
use of cosmetics and hairstyles; under "Costume and Accessories"
he includes comments on shoes and socks; and under "Cultivation of
Talents" he recommends that women study drama and fiction, learn
to play musical instruments, to sing, and to dance. All this training
will make them better companions for men.

His most incisive remarks are on charm in women:

> There is an ancient saying that "the power of exotic beauty fascinates."
> Exotic beauty means charm, although it has been commonly misunderstood
> as referring to "good looks" merely. Good looks, it should be understood,
> can never move us unless there is charm, and only then does beauty be-
> come fascinating and exotic. People who think that all beauties can fascinate
> people need only to stop to think why all the silk dolls and pictures of
> women can never move one, although probably their faces are ten times
> more beautiful than living women. Charm in a person is like the flame in a
> fire, the light in a lamp, and the luster in jewels. . . . For charm not only
> enhances beauty and attraction in women, it can make the old appear
> young, the ugly beautiful, and the dull become exciting. . . . Charm is
> something that comes naturally to a person and grows directly out of her
> personality. It is not something which can be copied from others, for charm
> imitated is beauty spoiled. . . .
> Some readers may ask, Is it true that charm can never be taught, for we
> say that one can even learn to be a saint or a sage? I can only say in reply
> that charm can be learned, but cannot be taught. If it again be asked, Why
> can't it be taught if it can be learned? my reply is that people without charm
> can learn it by living together with people who have it. They will acquire it
> by daily example and contagion, like reeds learning to grow straight in a
> field of hemp. It comes gradually and naturally and by a kind of invisible
> influence. To lay down so many rules for acquiring charm would be futile
> and, indeed, only makes for greater confusion.[50]

Closely related to women and feminine charm is sex. To Li, the
root of all happiness lies in sexual fulfillment. Though it is a boon
and offers many blessings to man, it can easily degenerate into a
curse and threaten man's physical and mental well-being: "Among
the places of pleasure, the foremost is the bedroom. Many who do
not know how to handle sex make it the festering ground of jealousy
and family discord, and the origin of disaster; then there are others
who indulge in it too much, ruining their health and incurring an
early death. It is certainly a problem. . . ."[51] He disapproves of
excessive sexual activities; advises abstaining from sex whenever a

person is depressed, hungry, cold, intoxicated, satiated, or weary in spirit or physically exhausted; and recommends moderate sexual activities during the first months of marriage or during cold winter nights and hot summer evenings.[52]

Born during the last years of the Ming regime, disappointed in the examination halls, and constantly beset by financial problems, Li never lost interest in life. A connoisseur of the art of living, he offers in *A Temporary Lodge* a comprehensive guide to dealing with the problems of human conduct. He stresses that happiness is not a ripe fruit that drops into one's mouth because of Lady Luck's special dispensation, but is rather something to strive for; and he maps out a commonsensical route by which he believes the average man and woman can reach that goal.

CHAPTER 2

Drama Without Sound
(Wu-sheng hsi)

I *Introduction*

FICTION, as it is understood in the West, was a late development in China. Although there were records of but few myths existing before 800 B.C., there were brief sketches of monsters with human attributes in the *Book of Hills and Seas (Shan-hai ching)*, in which fragmentary references are made to a superperson named the Queen Mother of the West (Hsi Wang-mu). In China's earliest book of poetry, *The Book of Songs (Shih-ching)*, there are descriptions of supernatural births of the founders of the Shang and Chou dynasties.

Following the collapse of the Han dynasty (220 A.D.), new stories of gods and ghosts became popular. Among the collections of such tales was *Strange Stories (Lieh-yi chuan)*, of uncertain authorship. Although this collection is now lost, some of its fantastic tales of ghosts and supernatural happenings have been preserved as fragments in other volumes. One motif is the relationship between supernatural beings and humans, often in the form of seductions.[1]

One of the earliest tales recording such a goddess-man relationship appears in *chüan* 1 of the *Dynastic History of the Wei (Wei-shu)*, completed in 554 A.D.:

[In the beginning,] the emperor Sheng-wu frequently led several thousand soldiers riding into the remote mountains. One day, all of a sudden, army equipment and provisions, together with some guards, descended from Heaven in the company of a beautiful girl. Being very much surprised, the emperor asked where she came from; she replied that she was the daughter of Heaven, and had received orders to be his wife. They slept together. When dawn came, she said she had to leave but instructed him to return to the same place in exactly one year. She left as swiftly as the wind and the rain. A year later, the emperor returned to the same place and found her there. She gave him a baby, saying: "This is our baby. Take good care of

him. Many generations will follow his line and they will all be emperors."
This baby was the founder of the Wei dynasty.[2]

Sketches like the above were mere outlines rather than full-
fledged stories. It was not until the T'ang dynasty (618–906 A.D.)
that such sketches developed into stories with sustained interest and
convincing characterization. As the earlier sketches or myths of
seduction evolved into longer romances, the gods and goddesses
assumed more human attributes. *The Fairies' Cavern (Yu-hsien
k'u)*, one of the pseudoautobiographical fairy goddess-man romances, was written by Chang Tsu (660–740). Setting out on an
official mission to the Northwest, a young scholar (presumably
Chang himself) stays at a mansion en route, where he meets two
girls, Tenth Sister and Fifth Sister. The trio feast and then amuse
themselves by writing naughty verses. As in all fairy-tale romances,
he leaves the following morning after a night of frolicking. As a story
it represents a significant step forward in the humanization of fairies
and divine beings. Vying with it for artistic achievement during the
T'ang period were Yüan Chen's (779–831) "The Story of Ying-ying";
Po Hsien-chien's (d. 826) "The Story of Madame Li"; Liu Kung-tso's
(770–850) "The Governor of Nan-ko"; Shen Ch'i-chi's (750–800) "Pillow"; and Tu Kuang-ting's (d. 918) "The Curly-bearded Man."
These and other stories made the T'ang a period of phenomenal
growth in fiction.[3]
    There were many reasons for this outburst of literary activity. The
T'ang dynasty was a time of economic prosperity, but perhaps, as
Lai Ming has said (based on a 1206 record of the Sung dynasty) the
most important reason was that

candidates for the civil service examination [during that time] could submit
short stories to officials in their effort to get official positions, as short stories
were thought to be a good way of showing the candidate's knowledge and
understanding of history and poetry and were a demonstration of a candidate's skill. This, incidentally, was the beginning of writers using their
imagination and perhaps personal experience in their writing, instead of
writing compositions which were based purely on ancient classics.[4]

Another reason was the rise of the illustrated text *(pien-wen)*. As
Buddhism became more popular with the people, Buddhist missionaries were trained in the art of using anecdotes and stories with
a moral to explain the esoteric *sutras* to the people. In an effort to

recruit more converts, missionaries developed ingenious devices to explain Buddhist texts, including illustrated narratives mixed with verses, descriptive passages, and allegories.[5] The narrator told "other stories as well, at first from the life of Buddha and of other Buddhist saints, but later no doubt stories of other origin."[6]

Some sixty years after the founding of the Northern Sung dynasty (960–1126), storytelling became a flourishing trade for professionals who specialized in different types of stories. Organized into guilds, many were born and raised in storytellers' families and developed their own stock of stories. Průšek comments: "All this was of great importance in the history of Chinese literature. For the first time there appeared in China a literary professional, for whom literature was not a diversion, . . . but a source of livelihood requiring a perfect mastery of the craft."[7] The vibrant Sung storytelling tradition continued throughout the Yüan and Ming dynasties. By the seventeenth century, storytellers' promptbooks *(hua-pen)* were quite popular, as evidenced by the existence of late Ming collections of short stories known as the *San-yen* and the *Erh-p'o*. The *San-yen* consisted of *Stories to Enlighten Men, Stories to Warn Men,* and *Stories to Awaken Men* and was compiled by Feng Meng-lung (1574–1646); and in the *Erh-p'o,* compiled by Ling Meng-ch'u (1580–1644), were *The First Collection of Amazing Stories* and *The Second Collection of Amazing Stories.*[8] Together the *San-yen* and the *Erh-p'o* served as the inspiration and models for many later short stories.

Despite the interest in fiction shown by the public, it was held in low esteem by orthodox scholars. They considered it "chitchat" or "small talk" of no consequence. Understandably, despite widespread popularity, the Sung storytellers' scripts and many of the Yüan and Ming novels were not listed or mentioned in official histories, though included in one or two bibliographical catalogs. This official neglect of fiction caused many novels and short stories to be published anonymously, and many writers preferred to conceal the fact that they wrote fiction. Professor John L. Bishop explains that "In an atmosphere where fiction in the colloquial language was considered almost a defilement of the long-treasured and esoteric art of writing, few members of the scholarly elite would risk being known as compilers of a version of popular fiction or as authors of a new specimen in any of its genres."[9]

A notable exception was Li Yü. Living at the time of the *San-yen*

and the *Erh-p'o* collections, he took his writing craft seriously, de-
claring with much pride: "I have always considered myself a writer
ever since I began to write. Though I dare not boast of the writing of
grandiose prose, I am somewhat skilled in writing poetry, drama,
and fiction."[10] In reality, he was a superior craftsman; the critic Sun
K'ai-ti has hailed him as one of the best Ch'ing short-story writers, a
view shared by many others.[11]

Li was well read and erudite. His reading supplied him with
many story ideas. From the story of the oil peddler in the *San-yen*
he developed his foolish hairdresser courting a heartless prostitute
in "An Official, Patronizing a Prostitute, Hears the Complaint of
Her Former Customer" *(Drama Without Sound,* Chapter 7). From
Feng Meng-lung's description of a crafty monk in his miscellaneous
jottings, Li devised the portrait of a swindler in "Tower of Self-
reformation." From other contemporary sources he borrowed the
incident of rebel troops auctioning off captured women in sacks as
described in "Tower of My Birth." And from an actual law case he
derived the story "Tower of Matrimonial Contest," which tells of
two inconsiderate parents simultaneously promising their two
daughters to four men.[12]

Perhaps a more important source than his readings was Li's own
colorful life. His large household with its numerous women gave
him ample opportunity to observe and to understand the different
shades of domestic tensions and discords, jealousies and squabbles;
his appreciation of the female and his interest in erotica made his
love passages eloquent and realistic; his brief but impressive wartime experience from 1644 to 1647 helped him explore human grief
and sufferings in times of civil disorder; and his constant and press-
ing woes deepened his understanding of human greed. More specifically, his fictional personae reflect his own experiences. For
example, the episode where, in a special contest, two women are
awarded to a scholar and live deer to other winners (as described in
"Tower of Matrimonial Contest") was based on fact. In 1646 the
official Hsü Ch'en-chang gave him a concubine, and he was also
given a live tiger as a special favor by Ch'ü Hsüan-ju, the assistant
prefect of Chin-hua.[13] Not only events but also characters were
drawn from Li's vivid life. Wei-yang Sheng, the Before Midnight
Scholar in *Prayer Mat of Flesh,* closely resembles Li as a young man;
the philosophical Yü Hao in "Tower of Three Dedications" is the
middle-aged Li, burdened with money problems and yet retaining

his ideals of life; and finally, Ku Ai-sou, the stubborn hermit in "Tower of Heeding Criticism," reflects an elderly Li wishing to withdraw from the strains of city living.[14]

Li's first collection of short stories was *Drama Without Sound,* probably published in 1657. It had four different editions, and their interrelationships with one another will be fully explored in Appendix I. The most popular edition, based on the copy in the *Sonkeikaku-bunko,* Tokyo, and reprinted in Taipei, in 1969, contains the following twelve stories.

II "*An Ugly Bridegroom, Fearful of Beautiful Women,
   Is Uniquely Blessed With Them*"

The theme of this story is nearly the same as that of Li's dramatic play, *Ordained in Heaven (Nai-ho t'ien):* an ugly man seeking a wife. Born with deformed facial features and an overpowering body odor, a rich man fares poorly with his first and second wives until his third wife persuades the other two women to join her in serving him. The simple plot is richly elaborated with description, comment, characterization, and differs from the traditional "talented-scholar and beautiful-woman" theme in its realism. Li says that it is not unusual for beautiful women to marry ugly men. Though he sympathizes with all such women and considers their sufferings the cruelest in the world, he counsels them to accept their fate and make the best of a less-than-ideal situation.

III "*A Handsome Man, Trying to Avoid Sex Scandals,
    Manages to Create Them*"

Despite the implications of the title, the story deals with the question of justice. In ancient China, the law was punitive, to be invoked whenever *li* or moral principles were violated. Moreover, it was primarily a penal code setting forth the penalties for different violations. Litigation was discouraged, for it was costly, and punishments were severe. Accused persons had no rights, received wretched treatment in prison, and were subjected to severe corporal punishment. Whipping, beating, and other tortures were frequently used to extort confessions from recalcitrant prisoners. Moreover, litigation brought disgrace not only to the parties directly involved but also to their families and even their clans. Consequently, people avoided trial and settled their disputes within the family; for in the courts, miscarriage of justice was commonplace.[15]

The reasons were obvious. First, since the commoners did not know the law, "the ruling class could manipulate it as it saw fit."[16] Its decisions were final and not subject to doubt or questioning by commoners. Second, the law applied only to commoners as the following quotation illustrates: "Proprieties [li] are not applicable to the common people; punishment is not applicable to the officials [ta-fu]."[17] Furthermore, throughout much of Chinese history, "the nobles and officials were not under the jurisdiction of the ordinary legal mechanisms and procedures. As a rule, the authorities had no right to arrest or investigate them unless permission to do so had been granted by the emperor."[18] Consequently, "Disputes between commoners on the one hand and officials on the other, entailed serious inequalities. . . . The higher the rank of the official, the more severe the punishment of the commoner."[19] Third, the law was a system of "ruling by man." Without clearly written laws to guide them, judges relied on their own wisdom and judgment in governing the people.

Under such a system, Li feels judges bear a heavy responsibility to see that justice is served, and his plea to them is direct and earnest: "All fair judges must be humble enough to care for their subjects and to never adopt the attitude that 'I have done right by Heaven and by man. And even if I misjudge a few cases, the people should not hold me responsible.' For attitudes like this have resulted in widespread miscarriage of justice and unjustifiably taken the lives of many."[20] In cases of homicide and adultery, Li stresses that judges must exercise extraordinary caution: "When judges are 99.99 percent certain of the facts, they must yet explore that .01 percent of doubt. Under no circumstances should they hastily reach a judgment and rule out the possibility of a later reversal."[21]

To return to "A Handsome Man . . . ," the story is a brilliant exposition of Li's argument. It illustrates and confirms his doctrine, serving as an exemplum in a lay sermon. The action originates with a nasty gossiping father filing a charge of adultery against his daughter-in-law and a neighboring scholar, citing as proof that a fan-drop given to her earlier was found in the possession of the scholar, whose study is separated from the girl's room only by a thin partition, as the two houses are adjoining. The judge mistakes the young woman's natural face coloring for the heavy makeup worn by disreputable women and concludes on the scantiest of evidence that the young people are guilty. Later the judge is accused by his own wife of cohabiting with his daughter-in-law, proof being that one of the young woman's shoes was found in his bedroom. Shamed and unable to clear her name, his daughter-in-law commits suicide. Puzzled and disturbed, the judge discovers accidentally that rats, prevalent in Szechwan province, had carried the incriminating shoe into his bedroom. Thus he is able to solve the fan-drop case as well. Were it not for this unusual set of circumstances, an irreparable damage would have been done to the accused.

Although Li writes about sympathetic and fair judges in other stories, he feels strongly that a judicial system based on the principle of "rule by man" and on other special privileges accorded the ruling classes has many drawbacks. As commoners have no way to redress their wrongs, "justice" too often depends on how lucky the accused is. Not a social reformer, Li stops short of advocating drastic changes in the system but·pleads for discretion and caution by those administering justice.

IV   *"With the Change of His Horoscope, the Misery of a* Yamen *Runner Ends and His Happiness Begins"*

Fortune-telling is the dominant subject of this story. Divination, as well as fortune-telling, has long been a part of Chinese culture and has affected the lives of both high and low. Fiction and the historical records abound with examples. Primarily, fortune-telling was the "reading" of either one's horoscope or one's physiognomy. The former is based on the eight cyclic characters for the year, month, day, and hour of a person's birth, and the latter the shape of a person's physiognomic features. For important matters such as betrothals, professional fortune-tellings are consulted who predict the future of the persons involved as well as the likely result of their relationship. Many potentially happy or disastrous marital alliances have been ruined or strengthened because of the supposed compatibility or noncompatibility of the two horoscopes. During Li's time, fortune-telling was taken very seriously. Pervading every aspect of daily life were auspicious and inauspicious days for weddings, funerals, for commencing building operations, for moving to a new residence, or for starting a journey. As an enlightened man, Li repeatedly points out the invalidity of fortune-telling and its potential dangers.

In the introductory tale, Li describes a grandfather who prides himself on his fortune-telling expertise. When his daughter-in-law is about to give birth to his first grandchild, he positions himself out-side her delivery room with a horoscope book in his hand. When birth is imminent, he checks the book and shouts that it is an un-lucky hour for the baby to arrive. Through the midwife, he instructs his daughter-in-law to delay the birth a little. Hurriedly, the daugher-in-law closes her legs and consequently suffocates the baby whose head had already appeared.

In the main story Chiang, a *yamen* runner or policeman, goes to a fortune-teller to have his horoscope analyzed, since he has had bad luck all his life. After the fortune-teller informs him that he will have more bad luck in the future, he sobs uncontrollably and begs the fortune-teller to do something for him. In jest, the fortune-teller writes him a new horoscope. With the new horoscope-paper in his sleeve, he returns late to the magistracy. Since he is late, the magis-trate flogs him for neglecting his duty and the horoscope-paper falls out of his sleeve. Curious, the magistrate looks at it and finds it to be identical with his own. Wondering how two people born at the same hour on the same day in the same month and year could have such different fortunes, the magistrate decides to befriend the runner. The magistrate's friendship is, of course, the turning point in Chiang's life. The uninterrupted misery of the past is replaced by a new way of life. He acquires a new wife and new clothes; he de-velops an interest in charitable deeds and becomes completely loyal to the magistrate. And when the magistrate is promoted to a higher rank, Chiang is made a petty official.

Li's purpose is not to extol Chiang's good luck or the magistrate's kindness, but to underline the farcical nature of horoscope reading. As we are all aware, a person's horoscope is presumably determined by his hour of birth and, therefore, can never be changed; con-sequently, the only intelligent person in the story seems to be the fortune-teller who has the bravado to change Chiang's horoscope for fun.

V   "*Loss of Fortune, the Fruit of Disaster,* *Turns Out to be the Root of Happiness*"

Continuing on the subject of fortune-telling, Li describes a mil-lionaire moneylender who has a unique method of lending money to borrowers. By "reading" each applicant's physiognomic features, he determines the amount of the loan to be granted. In the story, he correctly reads the fortunes of two young men who both become millionaries, one through hard work and the other through fate. Li achieves a happy ending by a series of contrived coincidences.

The convention of the happy ending does not deter Li from attacking the convention of fortune-telling by elaborating on the absurd actions of a moneylender who behaves more like a speculator than a banker; and Li achieves his purpose by clearly stating his own attitude against which the ridiculous actions of the lender can be measured.

VI *"A Female Ch'en P'ing Plots Seven Schemes"*[22]

An absorbing wartime narrative. With the heroine dominating the story, the action involves a series of episodes from the time Mrs. Keng is captured by outlaws until her reunion with her husband. An ordinary housewife, Mrs. Keng is known for her sharp wits. When outlaws near her hometown, she is confident that if captured she can outwit her captors and remain chaste. She tells her panicky husband not to worry about her but to leave and return home after the outlaws have left the area. She hides a few pieces of dirty cloth in her sleeves and instructs her husband to get her several croton beans from an apothecary before he leaves to hide.

When the town falls to the outlaws, she maintains her composure and willingly surrenders herself to a bandit chief. When he expresses the fear that beautiful as she is she might be taken from him by higher-ranking chiefs who are coming their way, she tells him that she will dishevel her hair and smear her face with coal ashes to make herself as ugly as possible. Thus the chief is assured of her sincerity.

That evening, without any prompting from him, she undresses and crawls into bed. As he begins his amorous advances, his sexual organ is blocked at "the gate" by a piece of tattered cloth. To explain the mystery, she remarks matter-of-factly that she is having her monthly period. Incredulous, he takes off the cloth "wrapping" for a firsthand examination and is greeted by the sight of blood and by a nauseating stench. Like a despondent warrior, he groans, vastly disappointed. In an apologetic tone, she comforts him: "If a woman has sex during menstruation, she will become ill later. If you don't want me to be your wife and insist on having sex now, I, of course, cannot stop you. But if you are serious about our future and having children, you had better wait a while. Besides, there are other women around. Why must you jeopardize my health?"[23]

Agreeing with her, the chief seeks his pleasures elsewhere and inquires if any of the women captives has any hidden wealth. Overhearing his inquiries, Mrs. Keng gets a new idea. Nonchalantly she asks if he has any savings and how much. He tells her that he has already saved more than two thousand ounces of silver and plans to become a law-abiding citizen as soon as he has accumulated three thousand more. Feigning hesitation, she murmurs: "I am afraid that you are not trustworthy. But if you are true to me, perhaps you can get ten thousand, let alone five." The chief's interest is aroused and he asks her to be more specific. Seemingly reluctant, she whispers to him: "With so many ears around, I can't tell you now, but I'll tell you more in private tomorrow night."[24]

The next evening, she still seems wary and says: "Men are mostly unreliable. You say you want to marry me, but I'm afraid that once you've gotten my money, you'll marry someone else. If you mean what you say, you must take a vow." Getting out of bed, he kneels down and makes the promise she insists on: "If I ever change my mind about you, I hope to die the death of a thousand knives." Helping him up, she finally takes him into her confidence: "My grandfather was a rich man and died recently. After his death, my late husband buried in the ground treasures amounting to ten thousand ounces of silver. If you dig it up, it should last us a lifetime. . . . Only my husband and I knew the whereabouts, and I saw with my own eyes that he was killed by your people. So no one knows about it but me."[25] Excited by the news, the chief grins with pleasure. Meanwhile they continue to travel with the other outlaws and captives.

Two days later, eager to resume his amorous advances, the chief asks her if her period has ended, and she answers affirmatively. Much gladdened he looks forward to a night of pleasure. When the engagement is about to begin, she groans in simulated pain and complains that a tumor has grown in her female organs, giving her chills and fever. Once more the thwarted warrior's penetration into "enemy territory" must be substituted by some superficial petting. As his hands wander hither and yon, she rubs some croton-bean oil on his "instrument," making it swell and consequently sexually useless. Craftily, she had earlier rubbed some croton-beans on herself in order to create the swelling in her pubic area.

Then one night they escape from the gang of outlaws. To ensure success, she persuades him to put his silver in a bag and submerge it in water somewhere, to be retrieved after they have dug up her husband's treasure. Further, she suggests that they dress as beggars to avoid detection by others when they are traveling.

The next day they journey toward her home. En route, while eating at a restaurant, she secretly crushes a few tiny croton beans and mixes them with his rice to induce diarrhea in him. Much weakened by his frequent bowel movements, he starts to have trouble walking. Patiently she helps him walk in the daytime and waits on him at night. Deeply moved by her sacrifices, he says to her: "Even though we are husband and wife in name, you have taken such excellent care of me that I can never fully repay you, not even in death."[26] On the third day, they stay at a temple, not far from her home. At dinner, she secretly mixes another mashed croton bean into his rice. Now he becomes so weak and sick that medication is needed. The next morning, claiming she must buy medication for him, she goes home and tells her husband to retrieve the chief's silver. It seems that her husband and other inhabitants have all returned to the town after the departure of the outlaws. Returning to the chief with the medicine, she nurses him back to health. When he appears well enough, she tells him she needs several shovels but runs home to check with her husband. After learning that everything has gone according to plan, she wants the chief arrested.

With several helpers, the husband arrests the chief. Sentenced to death by the local judge, the chief confesses before his execution: "When I first approached her, she had her period; when I approached her the second time, she had a poisonous lump. From then on I have been afflicted with diarrhea . . . ,"[27] thus clearing Mrs. Keng's name. Even though she could have disposed of him with her croton beans, she chose to let him live long enough to prove her chastity.

In terms of plot, this is one of the best stories in the collection. Its success lies in Mrs. Keng's successful execution of her schemes which depend, of course, on the ignorance and gullibility of her victim. Her every scheme appears logical and more "surprising" than the previous, and the resolution of the tension built up in the story helps the reader to achieve a state of equilibrium—something approaching calm of mind, in which all passion has been spent. As a story of intrigue, it is in the genre of Shakespeare's *Othello*, Ben Jonson's *Volpone*, Congreve's *The Way of the World*, and Wycherley's *The Country Wife*.

VII *"A Male Mother Meng Changes His Residence*
      Three Times to Protect His Foster Child"

In the introductory passages Li Yü ponders the origin of
homosexuality and its popularity; he maintains that homosexual
practices may be justified only when an elderly widower, too poor to
marry, uses it to satisfy his sexual needs, or when a young boy, too
poor to support himself, uses it to earn a living.

With homosexuality as the theme, Li Yü tells the story of how a
young boy, Jui-lang, bound by the principle of *pao* ("reciprocity"),
sacrifices himself for his male lover, Chi-fang. *Pao*, as explained by
Arthur H. Smith in *Proverbs and Common Sayings from the Chinese*
(1902), means that if "one person honors some other person a linear
(or other) foot, the other person should in return honor him ten feet.
Reciprocity means giving a horse in return for an ox, and that a case
of presents received is to be acknowledged by a case of presents in
return. . . ."[28] *Pao* has always been a favorite motif for Chinese
storytellers. The *San-yen* and the *Erh-p'o* collections both contain
stories extolling such virtues as unquestioning loyalty to the throne,
total obedience to the father, sacrifices of a wife for her husband,
and selfless friendship. Similarly, Li Yü develops the theme of *pao*
through the relationship of Jui-lang with his lover Chi-fang. Jui-
lang, a young boy, is "married" to the latter. Chi-fang treats Jui-lang
with tender loving care before and after "marriage" and regards
Jui-lang's father as his own. When Jui-lang's father dies, Chi-fang
mourns him with the proper rites as if he had lost his own father.
Deeply moved by Chi-fang's kindness, Jui-lang seeks to reciprocate
in full. When Chi-fang worries that the young man in maturing
might develop desires for the opposite sex, Jui-lang comforts him:
"While in life, we two share the same coverlet; and in death, we
shall share the same cave. Why do you have such doubts about my
fidelity?"[29] But Chi-fang remains unconvinced and sobs uncontrollably.

Unable to console his distraught lover, Jui-lang considers the
sacrifices that Chi-fang has made for him and makes a most unusual
decision: "All in all, his worries stemmed from the growth of my
sexual equipment. Why don't I cut off my testicles before they cause
friction between us? Eunuchs live in this world too; and there are
others who are without heirs. What if I get married and can't have
children? Now for repaying kindness, [*pao-en*], I shall take this

drastic act. My parents should not blame me for this."[30] Using a sharp razor he castrates himself. His reciprocity to his master-husband does not end there. Voluntarily he dresses as a woman, adopts female mannerisms, stays at home, learns needlework, and cares for Chi-fang's three-year-old motherless son.

But soon disaster follows. Envious of Chi-fang's good luck with his male-bride, other men with similar interests charge Chi-fang before the local magistrate with instigating the castration of a minor. The magistrate, also jealous of him, severely flogs Chi-fang who dies after telling Jui-lang: "After my death, others will have evil intentions toward you; therefore, you must leave this area. Bring up my son and educate him properly. If he succeeds in the examinations, I shall feel most honored and comforted in the other world."[31] Only sixteen years old himself, Jui-lang is left in charge of a three-year-old toddler and has to decide whether to continue his role as a woman or resume that of a man. In consideration of the youngster's welfare, he elects to act as though he were the lad's mother. To protect the child from the interest of homosexuals, he moves his residence three times and unselfishly devotes all his energies to his education. Li thus compares Jui-lang to the mother of the Confucian sage Mencius. She also moved her residence three times to give Mencius a better environment in which to grow up. As expected, Chi-fang's child succeeds in his scholastic endeavors and becomes a government official.

VIII "An Official, Patronizing a Prostitute, Hears the Complaint of Her Former Customer"

Li treats the subject of prostitution realistically in this story. Popular literature from T'ang to Ming times usually romanticized the relationship between scholars and courtesans in such tales as "The Story of Madame Li" by Po Hsien-chien or "Tu Shih-niang Angrily Sinks Into the River Her Hundred-Jewel Box" in the *Stories to Warn Men*.[32] In both stories, the courtesans are beautiful, talented, and highly skilled in music, dancing, and in carrying on clever conversation. In general, the courtesans in stories of this kind are interested in young scholars from good families with good prospects for future success. For when the young men passed their examinations and were appointed to positions in the public service, they would be able to redeem their loved ones from their keepers and either marry them or take them as concubines. However, these romantic tales meant little to commoners who had neither affluent parents nor prospects for future success. Then there appeared the story of a lucky oil peddler who won the love and wealth of a famed courtesan because he treated her with consideration and kindness.[33] As a story, it influenced many who wished to duplicate the good fortune of the oil peddler.

In the stories cited, the courtesans are described as being trustworthy, kindhearted, and love-oriented, and motivated by romantic traits. Li sought instead to present courtesans or prostitutes realistically. In the introductory tale he gives a detailed account of a Nanking prostitute named Chin. Beautiful and talented, her clientele includes the rich and the noble. Her charms easily captivate the soul of a young scholar from a good family. Determined to take her as a concubine as soon as feasible, he pays her fifty ounces of silver monthly, stipulating that she not receive other clients. Prior to returning home for a short visit, he again renews his pledge to her. In return, she vows complete fidelity to him. To test her loyalty, he asks friends to disguise themselves and attempt to patronize her. Without exception she rejects them all. Convinced of her fidelity, he returns the following year to fulfill his promise to her. Then he learns that she had died and left him a love-letter written in her own blood. The letter reaffirms her love for him and asks that she be buried properly. He mourns her death and gives her a proper burial.

Sometime later he is instructed in many useful sex techniques and aphrodisiacs by an instructor who, however, hesitates to teach him one last technique. Asked to explain his reluctance, the instructor says that the use of this technique had nearly killed a famed prostitute in Nanking. Much intrigued, the scholar presses for more details and is told that her name was Chin. Agitated, the scholar says:

"I heard that she had stopped receiving customers long ago. How did she happen to receive you?"

"Oh, yes, that was true on the surface. But in reality, she had a procuress who obtained customers for her every night."

"A few of my friends who had called on her all said that she had little interest in sex. And you claimed that your technique works best with women of strong sexual desires. If so, why did you apply it to her?"

"Young man, I have known a lot of women in my life. Many had strong desires, but none had a stronger sexual drive than Miss Chin. Your friends, perhaps inexperienced, only bored her. She told me she had no interest in novice lovers."

"Can you describe any of her physical characteristics?"
"Yes, she had a prominent scar below her belly-button but right above her private parts."[34]

The scholar asks no further questions, recognizing the scar as resulting from a cauterization she performed in token of fidelity to him on the eve of his departure from Nanking. He now knows that he had been completely duped by her.

In the story proper which follows the introductory tale, Li tells of an illiterate and pathetic hairdresser with grandiose illusions. He works out an arrangement with Sister Snow, a prostitute, and her madam. Both will be paid a sum of money over a period of years to redeem Sister Snow from the house. In addition, he will comb Sister Snow's hair every day and perform other chores around the house. In five years' time, after he has fulfilled all the agreed-upon conditions, the madam and Sister Snow both deny ever having made any agreement with him and insist that the money he has spent must be considered as the usual expenses incurred in visiting the house. He denies that he has ever touched Sister Snow, but his arguments fall on deaf ears. He seeks justice from the magistrate's court which offers him none; he seeks sympathy from friends and strangers who reward him with sneers and jeers. In utter desperation, he prepares a signboard listing his bill of grievances against Sister Snow and her madam and carries it on his back wandering in the streets, eliciting universal laughter from the onlookers. Then he stations himself outside the madam's house and recites his grievances to any incoming clients who will listen. None of these brings him any satisfaction and humiliation and anguish finally take their toll. His spirit departs from his body one night and grieves before one of Sister Snow's new patrons, a grain-transport official. In the end, the official rights the hairdresser's wrongs by helping him recover his money from the house. In elaborating on the story of the hairdresser, Li hopes to reveal the truth about prostitutes and to destroy whatever illusions people might have about them.

IX "The Father's Ghost Wreaks Revenge for the Son's Gambling Debts"

Li's purpose in this story is to warn his readers of the evils of gambling. He portrays in detail the life of a gambling broker named Wang Hsiao-shan. With some inherited wealth, Wang builds a house with a garden, invites rich young men to gamble there, and

draws a commission from the games arranged by him. Because he
never participates in the games he takes no risks and his income is
steady. One day he interests in his game a young man named Wang
Chu-sheng who comes from a hard-working and prosperous family.
Chu-sheng soon loses his family fortune, even its land and other
assets which can only be disposed of after his father's death. His
father finally dies, without knowing of these losses; and his mother
dies soon thereafter of a broken heart when she learns of them. After
burying his parents and paying off his gambling debts, Chu-sheng is
destitute and has to live off his father-in-law.

Unexpectedly, with only a few coming to his house to gamble,
Wang Hsiao-shan's business becomes less profitable than before.
One day a handsomely-clad stranger arrives with four fully-loaded
trunks and asks for a Wang Shao-shan. Impressed by the stranger's
apparent wealth, Wang claims to be Wang Shao-shan though he is
Wang Hsiao-shan and bids the stranger welcome. The stranger
identifies himself as Mr. T'ien (that is, Mr. Land) and expresses an
interest in a few friendly games, which Wang promptly arranges.
The stranger opens his trunks and shows Wang four thousand
ounces of silver to be exchanged for chips. After ten days of continu-
ous gambling, the stranger loses the equivalent of four thousand five
hundred ounces of silver, and before leaving Wang he writes a
promissory note for the extra five hundred ounces to come due in
three months. When the other players seek to cash in their win-
nings, Wang promises to cash in their chips as soon as he opens the
locked trunks. Who could guess that the silver left behind by the
stranger had turned into worthless piles of paper money inscribed
with Chu-sheng's name, the kind to be burnt for the use of departed
spirits? Wang realizes that he has been deceived by the ghost of the
young man's father. Responsible for the ghost's losses, Wang goes
bankrupt and soon dies.

Li puts the moral of the story as follows: "The winner and the
loser, unwilling to give up gambling, only enrich the broker. So in a
gambling house the loser courts annoyance, the winner gets a transitory pleasure, the spectator loses time, and the broker gets the
profit."[35] Even though Li uses a ghost to right the scales of justice,
his moral is convincing and compelling to the large unsophisticated
readership which has been conditioned to expect a moralistic ending
to a story of apparent evil. Tu Chün comments that it is a story that
should be read by children and parents alike.[36] The critic Chiang

Jui-chao adds: "The Fisherman of the Lake (Li Yü) is the author of a story of a ghost losing money, and his description of the gambling house is vivid and realistic. . . . the miraculous work of his pen. . . . The first part of the story deals with the evils of gambling, and the second, with revenge or retribution—filled with realistic descriptions, awesome to read. . . . Alas, many young masters are addicted to gambling and have destroyed their family names. Their numbers are countless.[37]

X *"By a Strange Bargain a Bodhisattva*
Transforms a Daughter Into a Son"

This is the satiric portrait of a niggardly merchant and his faithless dealings with a Tantric Bodhisattva Cundi. After contracting with the Bodhisattva in a dream to dispense four-fifths of his wealth so as to benefit the poor in return for a male heir, the merchant reneges on his agreement after learning that one of his concubines is pregnant. Who could guess that the baby, when born, would be hermaphroditic, possessing the organs of both sexes? Ignoring his tearful pleas, the Bodhisattva insists that the merchant fulfill the terms of their agreement. And only after the merchant disburses his money does the Bodhisattva transform the infant into a full-fledged son.

In addition to Li's humorous descriptions of the bargaining between the merchant and the Bodhisattva (who appears to be an equally shrewd bargainer), he underlines the importance of the family lineage issue. Precisely because of the merchant's miserly nature, his willingness, however reluctant, to part with most of his wealth is a significant indication of how much a traditional Chinese would sacrifice to have an heir to carry on the family line.

XI *"Replacing the Concubine With the Wife*
Is the Marvelous Work of the Divine"

Jealousy between wives and concubines is the subject of the story. Li begins with random comments: *"Ts'u* [vinegar] is a good condiment. When the ancients gave names to things they meant well. Of the seven daily necessities, *ts'u* is indispensable. . . . *ts'u* used properly in cooking makes the diner taste its sweetness but not its bitterness. . . . If a woman fights for what she should not, takes what she should not, and is interested solely in herself, she is like a cook who has a special fondness for *ts'u.* And when such a person cooks, she has no regard for any other palate but her own. When she should use salt and soy, she uses *ts'u* instead. And the diner can only taste its bitterness."[38] Thus, *ts'u* connotes jealousy and to use *ts'u*, or vinegar, is to be jealous. To Li, a small amount of jealousy is both intrinsic to human nature and harmless. But when it grows out of proportion, it breeds disaster.

In the introductory tale, a concubine has monopolized her husband for ten years, but she feels deserted when he spends one night with the first wife. In anger the concubine sets fire to the family pigsty, and tries thus to rout him from his wife's bed. But instead she burns down the whole neighborhood. In the main story, a concubine, jealous of her husband's first wife, tries in every way to slander her. Every such effort fails and she tries to poison the first wife. And when that too fails, she tells malicious lies about the wife to the husband. Gullible by nature, he believes these lies and banishes his first wife to her utter misery. Having no way to prove her innocence, the wife prays to the divine. Her prayers are answered and whenever the concubine sleeps with the husband, she is transported to a pigsty and replaced in bed by the wife. Possessed by evil spirits, the concubine finally confesses her wicked machinations. The story underscores Li's concern with the spark of jealousy and its igniting into a uncontrollable conflagration.

XII   "A Son and a Grandson Abandon the Ancestral Corpse and the Servant Arranges the Burial"

This well-developed story has two separate plots. The first emphasizes children's filial infidelity and the second the loyalty of a servant. A prosperous merchant named Shan Lung-ch'i has a grandson, Yi-sheng, by his deceased first son, and a young son, Shan Yü, born to him late in life. Close in age, the two are like brothers. Having been spoiled by Lung-ch'i, they do poorly in scholastic work but well in everything else. Feeling old, Lung-ch'i takes the two on a trip to acquaint them with his business. The two complain bitterly about discomfort on the road and are soon sick. Lung-ch'i nurses them back to health, but the effort exhausts him and he himself becomes seriously ill. Believing that death is near, he bares his thoughts to them:

Even though I may die in a strange land, it is almost like dying at home since you two are here to take care of everything. After I die, use the money

you collect from our customers to take my casket home. . . . I have something else to tell you, although I shouldn't. But if I don't tell you now, I'm
afraid that I might not be able to tell you later when my condition becomes
critical. I have buried several pots of silver back home. When you get back,
dig them up to buy land or to invest them in business. . . .[39]

When the two hear about the buried treasure, they become
feverish with greed. While Lung-ch'i hangs on to the last threads of
life, they grow edgy and suspicious of each other's intentions. One
day Yi-sheng disappears and goes home without informing either his
uncle or his grandfather. Meanwhile, Shang Yü muses to himself:
"My nephew has returned home and will undoubtedly dig up and
take the silver, leaving none for me. Even if I ask for my share, he
will not give it to me. There is no evidence of what father told us nor
proof of the situation. Shall he get everything and I, nothing?
Father's final arrangements have been made. . . . If I tell him what I
intend to do, he will stop me."[40] So he also rushes home the next
morning, deserting his dying father in a strange land. By allowing
greed to prevail over all other considerations, including filial piety,
the son and grandson court catastrophe. Predictably they receive
swift and just punishment. In a fist fight between them over the
silver, Shan Yü is killed instantly, and Yi-sheng later dies in jail,
having been sentenced to death by a judge.

The second plot centers on Pai-shun [a name which means a
hundred obediences], the bonded servant of old master Shan. Like
Jui-lang in "A Male Mother Meng" he, too, is bound by the principle of *pao* or reciprocity which applies to social relations of all types,
such as those between ruler and subject, father and son, husband
and wife, teacher and student, master and servant, and among
friends in general. Everyone should subscribe to the Mencian concept of *yi* or doing what is appropriately correct. And the human
being of supreme virtue always treats others correctly, regardless of
how they treat him.

Though Pai-shun has served his master Shan loyally for many
years and has gained the latter's confidence, he refuses to consider
being released from his bondage, giving his reasons as follows: "In
my previous life, I incurred many debts. Consequently, I was made
a servant in this life so that I can repay these debts. I intend to slave
for my master in this life. If I steal from him or cheat him, I will only
incur more debts which will have to be paid in the next one. If my

master has treated me meanly, I might have a reason to consider
redemption. But he has treated me like a son. How could I ever
treat him unfeelingly?"[41]

Thus when his master is abandoned in a strange land by his own
flesh and blood, Pai-shun rushes to him and attends to his needs.
Grateful for the help, Shan informs him that in his will he has
bequeathed to him all the money from the business' accounts re-
ceivable. He accepts the arrangements with apparent pleasure, just
to please his master. However, soon after the master's death, he
burns the will and explains his actions to others on the principle of *li*
or propriety: "There is an ancient saying that 'If the emperor wants
his subjects to die, they must die; if a father wants a son to die, he
must die.' Have you ever heard of a servant haggling with his master's family over money? My master wrote his will when he was
angry. . . . Were he alive today he would regret his decision. It was
better that I burned the will. . . ."[42]

He escorts his master's casket home. Upon learning that his
young masters, the son and the grandson, have both died, one in a
fist fight and the other in prison, he buries all three of them in the
same cemetery. Then one night his master appears to him angrily in
a dream: "You are a sensible man. Why did you do something so
unreasonable? You knew those two [his son and grandson] are my
enemies. They made me angry every day. And if you don't move
their graves, I will go elsewhere."[43] Pai-shun wakes up realizing
that the hatred between the master and his heirs has gone on un-
abated. Obediently, he reburies the young heirs elsewhere.

Then, strangely enough, the grandson appears to Pai-shun in
another dream pleading: "You know my uncle died in a fist fight
with me. Now we are buried right next to each other; he acts as my
enemy all the time. Would you please bury me elsewhere?"[44] Still
obedient, Pai-shun separates his two young masters and helps their
wives to remarry. Unwilling to see his old master heirless, he erects
a family altar and regards himself as the adopted heir of his master.

XIII   *"The Abandoned Wife and the Concubine Remarry
and the Maidservant Becomes the Child's Mother"*

The loyalty of widows is the central theme of the story. Scholar
Ma has a wife, a concubine, and a maidservant. When he is
twenty-nine years of age, his concubine gives birth to a son. But
soon Ma becomes critically ill. Thinking that death is near, he sum-

mons the three women to his bedside and asks what they will do should he die. His wife and concubine swear they would remain widows; the maidservant replies that if the family needs her she will stay, otherwise she sees no point in there being three celibate women in one family. Surprised and disappointed by her answer, he treats her coolly after his recovery.

Soon, Ma leaves home to practice as a physician in a different town; sometime later, it is reported that he is dead. Without losing any time, his wife and concubine both remarry, leaving his son with the maidservant. She cares for him for many years until Ma triumphantly returns, having successfully competed in the state examinations. Later, hearing that their former husband has returned as an important official, the wife commits suicide and the concubine dies of unmitigated grief. The maidservant's loyalty is rewarded by her being elevated to the position of first wife with full honors and privileges. Li's purpose, of course, is to demonstrate that the continued celibacy by widows should not just consist of verbal promises but of actual deeds.

The story is in some ways similar to Shakespeare's *King Lear.* Ma's exacting promises on his "deathbed" from his women; his wife and his concubine's promise of loyalty; and their later "betrayal" of him are reminiscent of King Lear's demanding the love of his three daughters, of Goneril and Regan's avowal of love, and their subsequent betrayal of him. On the other hand, Ma's maidservant's uncommitted but truthful answer is similar to Cordelia's vow to love her father according to her "bond; no more nor less."[45] Ma's recognition of his maidservant's true love for him and her dedication to the family is also comparable to Lord Walter's recognition of Griselda's true virtues as told so brilliantly in Chaucer's "The Clerk's Tale."[46]

CHAPTER 3

Twelve Towers (Shih-erh lou)

WHILE *Drama Without Sound* was published before 1658, *Twelve Towers* was completed either in that year or shortly afterward, as it bears a 1658 preface written by Tu Chün. The work is also known as *Famous Sayings to Awaken the World (Chüeh-shih ming-yen)*, and it continues to be the only collection of short stories written by Li Yü which remained in circulation in China.[1]

I *"Tower of Joining Reflections"*

Similar to the romantic comedy as developed by Shakespeare and his Elizabethan contemporaries, "Tower of Joining Reflections" has a handsome hero, beautiful heroines, obstacles to the achievement of romantic fulfillment, and a happy ending. In addition to the traditional "talented-scholar and beautiful-woman" theme, it contains both surprises and suspense and impresses the reader with the ingenuity with which the happenings in the beginning and middle of the story contribute to its resolution. The story is set in the *Chih-cheng* era of the Yüan dynasty (1341–1367); T'u and Kuan, brothers-in-law who live in Ch'ü-chiang in Kwangtung province, are bitter enemies. They are antipodal personalities: T'u is lax in moral attitudes while Kuan is extremely strict. To avoid contact with the T'u family, Kuan erects high walls along the common boundary of their properties, leaving two separate pavilions built above water in their backyards as the closest link between them.

T'u has a son named Chen-sheng, and Kuan, a daughter named Yü-chüan. The two look almost like identical twins because their mothers, who are sisters, also look very much alike. Years earlier, when the two families were still friends and Chen-sheng and Yü-chüan were infants, they lived together in one house and hardly anyone could tell them apart. But now, as adults they have had no opportunity to become acquainted. Then, one day, accidentally, both go to their water pavilions at the same time. The breeze being very mild, the two houses are clearly reflected in the water. Suddenly, Yü-chüan imagines that she sees her own self reflected in the water of the other house. After some initial moments of bewilderment, she realizes that it is the reflection of Chen-sheng, her cousin, a person whom she has heard about but does not remember ever having met. Almost simultaneously, Chen-sheng realizes that he is looking at Yü-chüan's reflection in the water. Though separated, they fall in love.

After giving his reader a description of a picture-book romance, Li Yü presents Kuan as the major stumbling block to the young lovers' future happiness. When Mr. Lu, a matchmaker, speaks on behalf of Chen-sheng, Kuan expresses how he feels about Chen-sheng's father and the marriage proposal by writing the following words on his table top: "Our interests and personalities are different and the conflict has existed for a long time. I have, in fact, been thinking about terminating the friendship completely, so it is impossible to talk about a marriage-alliance. If he wants the relationship to be more than it is now, it would be like dreaming dreams in a dream!"[2]

Finding it impossible to persuade Kuan, T'u arranges for his son to marry Mr. Lu's daughter instead, keeping his son in the dark about his plan. And it is Yü-chüan who first hears of the news. In a sorrowful and angry letter she condemns Chen-sheng for his infidelity. Rushing to his father, Chen-sheng demands that his engagement to Chin-yün, Lu's daughter, be nullified or he will commit suicide. His father apologizes to Lu and explains why the engagement has to be annulled. After much discussion Lu agrees to find a new husband for his daughter. However, when Chin-yün learns of this new development, she feels betrayed and aggrieved by her father as her maids speculate how nice it would have been were she to marry Chen-sheng. Soon she becomes seriously ill.

Li builds up the emotional conflicts among the characters so that Lu finds himself in an untenable position. His original role as a matchmaker between two irreconcilable families has developed into a most serious situation: his own daughter is heartbroken; the stubborn Mr. Kuan refuses to consider Chen-sheng; Chen-sheng demands justice from T'u and from him; Yü-chüan secludes herself in her quarters, since she has no way of consummating her union with Chen-sheng; and Chin-yün feels betrayed and unwanted. In the tradition of storytellers, Li Yü suddenly endows Lu with the wisdom necessary to solve the problem: "Why don't I arrange for both girls to marry the boy at the same time? . . . I'd have to keep old Kuan in the dark and let him play the villain. When it's all over, he will know the whole story. By then the raw rice would have been cooked into *fan*, and there is nothing he can do about it. But still which girl should be Chen-sheng's first wife and which, the second? . . . Oh, well, they could very well call each other 'sister!' "[3]

To implement his plan, he reveals to Chen-sheng's father his course of action: "Your honorable relative is the stubbornest of men. . . . As you know, I have no son, and Kuan has often advised me to adopt one. I plan to tell him that I have adopted one and wish to have his daughter as my new son's wife. Most likely he will accept the proposal. After he agrees, I will tell him that my daughter will marry your son on the same day. . . ."[4]

As expected, Kuan agrees to the proposal and the wedding takes place in Mr. Lu's house. The story ends as happily as a fairly tale:

> The two girls are like the hydrangea flowers leaning by
>   the tree of jade;
> They are like two light clouds by the bright white moon.
> With that couple who were born on the same day, it is
>   hard to tell who is older or younger;
> With this couple, who look alike, it is hard to tell who
>   is the bride and who the groom.
> . . . .
> Unparalleled happiness! Truly they are three immortal
>   spirits.[5]

II *"Tower of Matrimonial Contest"*

As marriages in ancient China were always arranged by parents and determined by their self-interest or wisdom, many marriages turned out to have been arranged not in Heaven but in Hell. Some parents arranged their children's marriages so casually that there was no possibility that their children could be happy. Not infrequently a daughter was first engaged to Chang San (or Tom) and later to Li Ssu (or Dick). This resulted in endless quarrels and turned what should have been a happy occasion into a morass of petty lawsuits.

Among Li's short stories, "Tower of Matrimonial Contest" treats this subject fully. It begins with an introductory *tz'u* poem to the tune of "As in a Dream: A Song" (*Ju-meng ling*):

> One saddle for one horse,
> One daughter for one son-in-law,
> Irresponsible promises are a breach
>   of the five human relationships.
> None should change the promise of betrothal;
> The wish to be paired is hard to fulfill.[6]

In the introductory passages, Li elaborates on parental responsibility toward their children's marriages:

Which parents would not want their children prosperous and their sons-in-law prominent? If parents break their earlier promises of betrothal, it is because of their love for their daughters and their desire to have them marry better, and it is not because of any evil intent. This bit of snobbishness is inherent in all parents with eligible daughters. But the exercise of such discretion must be done before, and not after, having made any commitments. At that time, if they were truly snobbish, they should reject offers from impoverished families and wait for those from rich or important families. . . . But if they changed their mind after having made commitments, they would then create many problems for their daughters. . . .[7]

In the story proper, Li describes the making and breaking of marriage promises by a pair of inconsiderate parents who clearly abuse the sacred privileges of parenthood. A fish jobber named Ch'ien Hsiao-chang and his wife are not known for their marital harmony. Quarreling frequently and bitterly over differences of opinion, they are unwilling to compromise on any issue. They have two beautiful daughters and soon receive many different wedding proposals from matchmakers. Since their family discord is well known, the matchmakers believe that it would be more practical, if less conventional, to approach Mrs. Ch'ien first; they reason that she would be impossible to handle if angered and that she seems to have the more decisive voice in family matters. Snubbed by the matchmakers, Mr. Ch'ien resents them and promises to marry his daughters to the first two young men who ask him directly. At the same time, Mrs. Ch'ien promises the daughters to two others. Consequently, as a result of the lack of consultation between husband and wife, the girls are engaged to four men and wedding gifts are pouring into the Ch'ien household like spring showers. Meanwhile, both Mr. and Mrs. Ch'ien wonder, separately, where the two extra sets of gifts are coming from; their bewilderment is replaced by shock and anger when they learn the truth.

The case is finally brought before a local judge. Sympathetic to the plight of the two girls, the judge devises an examination to find who is truly deserving of the girls. The winner is scholar Yüan who writes the two best essays and is duly awarded both girls. Later, after passing the provincial examination with flying colors, Yüan becomes a Hanlin Academician and a high official in the government. The judge, having won a fine reputation for his decision in the case of the twin sisters, is also moved to the capital where he is appointed a scrutinizing secretary of the military division. Li concludes the story with an ancient proverb: "Only people with like minds can appreciate each other."[8] In this case the proverb applies, of course, to the judge's appreciation of both the girls and Yüan.

III   *"Tower of Three Dedications"*

Merciless exploitation of one's neighbors is the theme of this story. Mr. T'ang and his son are consummate exploiters. Rich and calculating, they believe that expensive homes cost too much to maintain and are, in addition, subject to the risk of fire; that fine clothing would be borrowed by friends; and that delicious food would tempt uninvited relatives and others to join them at their table. Therefore, instead of building their own dream house, they deliberately plan to exploit their neighbor, a Mr. Yü, who is building an estate nearby. Yü incurs so many debts in its construction that he must put it up for sale and the T'angs "reluctantly" examine it, spending most of their time finding fault. After hard bargaining, they purchase the estate from Yü for less than a fifth of the asking price. The sale includes everything on the property except one three-story pagodalike building called "San-yü lou" or "Tower of Three Dedications," which Yü keeps for his personal use.

After remodeling their new estate, the T'angs remain displeased, since their friends suggest that they should have bought San-yü lou as well. Obsessed with acquiring it and faced with Yü's refusal to sell, the T'angs try legal technicalities to evict Yü and his family. That too fails and they put a curse on Yü, wishing him an early death. Finally, they persuade Yü to sell them San-yü lou but only after allowing their greed to stifle what few instincts of kindness and generosity toward others they have.

If the T'angs are evil, then Mr. Yü is a man to be admired. An idealist, his credo of life is simple, centering on the house in which he lives, the bed in which he sleeps, and the coffin to which he will eventually retire. When he runs into financial difficulties, he has no second thoughts about selling his dream house to his archenemies who have consistently exploited him. His friends complain about his poor business acumen, but he tells them:

I sold it for my own sake. Can't you see that I am an old man with a very young son? How can I be sure that my son would not sell it after my death? . . . It is better that I sell it now and people would at least feel sorry for my son. This is only a minor reason. What if I soon die, leaving a very young son and a stubborn wife who refuses to sell it? After repeated frustrations, the T'angs might then resort to evil means to get rid of my offspring. At that time I'm afraid that not only my property would never be redeemed, my son's life would also be in jeopardy.[9]

His logic fails to convince his friends, but his farsightedness serves as an incentive to his young son who later becomes a high government official and recovers the entire estate from the T'angs without bearing any grudge against them.

Apart from portraying two contrasting personalities and the themes of exploitation and greed, Li Yü wrote the story out of his own personal experience. Its two introductory poems are identical with two others collected in his *Sayings of One School*.[10] The poems record his sad experience of having to sell his Yi-shan pieh-yeh in 1647, a house that he had carefully planned for and designed, at a sacrificial price. The recovery of the estate in the story by Mr. Yü's son expresses Li Yü's own dream of having a son who would distinguish himself in the examination halls and recover that which he himself had lost. Lastly, Mr. Yü's son's gentle treatment of the T'angs is consistent with Li Yü's own belief that "good and evil will each be appropriately rewarded and punished sooner or later. It is simply a matter of time."[11]

IV "Tower of Summer Comfort"

Like "Tower of Joining Reflections," "Tower of Summer Comfort" is a love story. It portrays a lover's confrontation with his snobbish prospective in-laws and his eventual success, and illustrates Li Yü's handling of dramatic conflicts within a story. A scholar, Ch'ü Chi, wishes to marry Chan Hsien-hsien, the daughter of a country squire. When Ch'ü proposes to her father, the latter replies that he cannot make any decision until after the autumnal provincial examination. Having passed, Ch'ü is told to put his proposal to Hsien-

hsien's two brothers who are officials in the capital. When he arrives in the capital, the two brothers inform him that they will not consider anyone until after the imperial examination. Again, Ch'ü passes, but his score is not good enough to place him among the senior scholars. The two brothers then inform him that two other successful candidates from their district have also asked to marry Hsien-hsien, and that the names of all three have been sent to their father for his final decision.

Mr. Chan, the father, decides that the only fair solution would be to ask his daughter to draw lots. On the appointed day he writes the names of three suitors on pieces of paper which he puts in a gold vase. After the proper rites, Hsien-hsien, having been led to believe that Ch'ü is an immortal, "confidently" draws a piece of paper, only to find the name of another suitor written on it. Shocked, she wonders where Ch'ü's magic power has gone. Meanwhile, assuming that the die has been cast, Chan hurries her to make her ritual bows of gratitude before the family deity. Here arises the first crisis in the story. Should she obey her father and thus seal her fate?

The following is how Li unfolds the heightening drama:

. . . Hsien-hsien . . . knelt before Mr. Chan and pleaded in a solemn tone: "Your daughter has something very important to tell you but is afraid to speak. But if she doesn't say it now, her happiness will be ruined."

"What could be so difficult for you to say in front of your own parent? Speak up," replied Mr. Chan.

Hsien-hsien stood up and said: "Your child had a dream last night in which her late mother appeared. She said, 'Among the three men there is only one who should be your husband. . . .' When your child pressed her for the name, Mother only gave his surname and not his other names, and it was Ch'ü. . . . Who could know that I would choose the name of another and not the right one? That was why I was hesitating, unwilling to offer thanks to the deity. . . ."

After some hesitation, Mr. Chan said: "What nonsense! If your mother's spirit is all knowing, why didn't it appear to me in a dream instead of to you? If what you said is true, then it should have protected the right one at the lot-drawing time, and how did you choose another? This is utter nonsense, and I don't believe a word of it."

Hsien-hsien instantly replied: "Whether you believe me or not depends on you. As for your child, she relies solely on her mother's word and will marry no one but Ch'ü."

After hearing all that, Chan exploded and said: "You don't obey your living father but use your deceased mother to intimidate me. What you have been saying is absurd, and how do I know that you didn't fabricate the whole story to cover up some illicit affair of yours? Nevertheless, wait until I pray to her, asking her if what you said is true. If it is, she should appear to me in a dream. If within three nights, I don't get the dream, not only will I not allow you to marry Ch'ü, I will also investigate the whole matter. . . ."[12]

How does Li solve this second crisis with Chan threatening his daughter with severe punishment if he fails to have a dream-visitation from his late wife within three nights? First, Hsien-hsien writes to Ch'ü and receives a note from him which bolsters her confidence in confronting her father. When her father tells her three days later that he has received no response from her mother, she calmly replies that her mother appeared to her again saying that she could not approach Chan because Chan was always in the company of concubines, and that her mother told her something else which she hesitates to repeat lest it frighten him. Intrigued, he presses her for details. Then she tells him that her mother told her that he had burned a written prayer immediately after it was written, and further that her mother had told her what it had said. He then asks her to tell him what the prayer said. With complete confidence, she recites word for word. Finally convinced of her honesty, Chan allows her to marry Ch'ü.

What did Ch'ü tell Hsien-hsien in his letter of instructions? He informed her of the contents of her father's written prayer. Li Yü tells his reader that Ch'ü had found out by acquiring "superhuman" powers through a telescope he had purchased in an antique store. Using it he could see far and wide. It was through the telescope that he first saw a group of mischievous naked girls bathing in a pond and, later, their mistress, Hsien-hsien; using it, he learned all that took place in Hsien-hsien's house; and it ultimately enabled him to win his wife. Indeed, Li Yü could very well have been the first Chinese writer to use a telescope to solve a lover's problems.

V *"Tower of Self-reformation"*

"Tower of Self-reformation," as the title suggests, obviously has a moral: that an evil man, when reformed, will be coveted by God. Apart from its moral, the major interest of the story lies in the use of the trickster motif, popular in both folklore and literature. In folklore the trickster appears as Br'er Rabbit, Bugs Bunny, the

coyote of the American Indian, Reynard the Fox, or as the monkey
in the Chinese classical novel, *Pilgrimage to the West (Hsi-yu chi).*
In literature, the trickster appears as Til Eulenspiegel, Colonel Sel-
lers, and Gully Jimson and in such short stories as Mark Twain's
"The Man That Corrupted Hadleyburg," William Faulkner's "Spotted Horses," Ring Lardner's "Haircut," and others.[13]
    Li Yü's trickster is energetic and clever as are all successful
swindlers. Li tells the reader that:

During the *Yung-lo* years [1403–1424] of the Ming dynasty, there was a
swindler of incredible talent. No one knew his name, where he came from
or what he really looked like. There were always rumors that so-and-so had
been swindled, and that the swindler was most recently spotted in the
South. Who would know that he had for some time operated out of the
North? The victims had him arrested time and time again, but he had to be
released every time because of the lack of evidence. Moreover, being an
expert in the use of makeup, he could change his appearance at will. . . .[14]

    When P'ei is young, his parents, petty thieves themselves, coun-
sel him:

To be a successful swindler, . . . you must have the shrewdness and cleverness of Messrs. Sun and P'ang, the bravery of Meng Pen and Hsia Yü, the
persuasiveness of Su and Chang, and the flexibility to adapt yourself to
every situation, however unexpected, for otherwise you will, sooner or
later, be caught red-handed. Swindling is very unlike our family trade.
There isn't much risk being caught while stealing in the dark. We advise
you most strongly to follow in our footsteps and to become a petty thief.[15]

    But his parents' advice falls on deaf ears. P'ei insists that he has
swindling talents. To test their son's skill, his parents, who are
upstairs in their house, ask if he can get them to go downstairs. He
shakes his head and says: "but if you were downstairs, I could get
you to go upstairs." His parents then go downstairs to see if he could
do so. Smilingly, he announces his victory: "You are now downstairs, are you not? Need I say more?"[16]
    With his credentials established, P'ei scores many triumphs, each
better than the one before. A generous person, he befriends people
of all social classes. When prostitute Su expresses to him her desire
to become a nun, he purchases an estate and divides it into two
parts, with the building on the right side to be converted into a

Buddhist temple for her (whom he renames Pure Lotus) and the others to be used as places to store his spoils.

At this point in the story Li Yü introduces a turning point in P'ei's life. Among the buildings on the left side, there is one with an old votive tablet with a horizontal inscription: "Kuei-chih lou" or "Hall of Retirement." But when P'ei moves into it, this name seems to have been changed into "Kuei-cheng lou" or "Hall of Reverting to Purity." P'ei soon discovers that the extra stroke on top of the character "chih" [making it "cheng"] has been made by dirt carried there by swallows. Convinced that Heaven had willed him to become a good man, he changes his name to "Kuei-cheng" or "Self-reformation" and ordains himself a Taoist priest.

The story could have ended here, had Li Yü's purpose been to describe the moral reformation of a swindler, but Li Yü's real emphasis seems to be on P'ei's clever manipulation of others even after his self-proclaimed moral reformation. One day P'ei tells Pure Lotus of his intention to build two separate temples, one Buddhist and one Taoist, for worship. When asked how he can accomplish that, he replies that he is going home to bury his parents and will return in a year and that by that time all the construction work will have been completed. A few days later he invites a craftsman to remodel one of the estate's eighteen images of Arhat and soon leaves for an unknown destination with his disciples.

Six months later, a retired official and a rich merchant visit Pure Lotus, each volunteering to build a separate temple on the compound grounds. Pure Lotus, stunned by the offer, cannot understand why and how these two men, one from the Hunan-Hupeh region and the other from Shansi, happen to have the same inclinations simultaneously. She asks for explanations.

The retired official replies that he had been visited by an immortal disguised as a human and told that a temple had to be built in this area before a certain date, and that he should be the one to do it. Not impressed by the statement, the merchant asks the retired official how the latter could be sure that it was not a pretender from Pure Lotus's temple. Then the official continues to tell his story:

When he first came to see me and claimed to be an immortal, my servants refused him admittance into the house. He then wrote four characters on my outside door, "Hui tao-jen pai" meaning "Hui, the Taoist priest, sends his regards." Before he left, he said to my servants, "I am an old friend of

your master. When he sees these characters on the door, he will understand. Tomorrow I will call again at the same time. Even if you don't tell
him I have been here, he will come out himself to greet me. It is useless for
you to try to stop me." After he left, the servants scrubbed the door with hot
water for several hours, but the characters could not be erased. Then they
told me what had happened. . . . Later I hired a carpenter to plane the
door. . . . the characters could not be expunged.[17]

After taking a breath, the official describes his meeting with the
immortal the next day. It seems that the immortal carried a sharp
and shiny sword on his back, and a small bottle-gourd about three
inches long and one inch wide on his waist. When the official requested the immortal to take off his sword, the latter inserted the
blade into the bottle-gourd and within a quarter of an hour the blade
disappeared within the gourd and the sword handle became its cork.
After that demonstration by the immortal, the official had no further
doubts.

He then asks the merchant his reasons for being there. The merchant replies that he did not witness any miracles, but that a Buddhist elder had been sitting sedately and contemplatively outside
the merchant's door every day for a long time. The elder explained
about the temple's construction but requested no cash, so the merchant entered the amount of contribution in the elder's collection
book. Now he wonders if the elder had collaborated with the official's immortal to deceive them both, and demands an explanation
from Pure Lotus.

Pure Lotus vehemently denies knowing anything about these incidents. After some discussion, the official suggests to the merchant
that they should build the temples as they originally intended. After
a night of rest, the two stroll leisurely around the compound to look
for a proper site to begin construction. Suddenly, they are visibly
shaken, for it seems that they have found an Arhat image which
looks just like the elder who had sat for so many hours outside the
merchant's house. When the merchant approaches the Arhat image,
he finds a book in its hands which looks like the collection book
presented to him by the elder. Looking through the book, he finds
his name written in his own handwriting on a certain page.

The merchant has no more doubt about his mission. He, too, has
met an immortal one disguised as a Buddhist elder. Assured, he and
his new friend personally supervise the construction of the two

temples. Upon their completion, they meet a priest whose appearance and demeanor is more immortal than human. When questioned by the two, the priest answers that his name is Kuei-cheng, that he has just returned from burying his parents, and that he will be in charge of the temples. The official honors Kuei-cheng as an immortal, asks to be accepted as a disciple and be given a Taoist name. Similarly, the merchant reveres Pure Lotus as another immortal and begs to be given a Buddhist name which he can pass on to his son later, if he is to have one.

From then on, Kuei-cheng and Pure Lotus dedicate themselves to worship and salvation. Then one day she asks him how he managed to get the two temples built. He says he sent two disciples, one disguised as an immortal to the Hunan-Hupeh region, and the other as a Buddhist elder to Shansi, while he himself went home. As for the miraculous events, the ink used to write the characters on the door contained turtle urine. The urine etched itself deeply into wood and nothing could remove it. The sword blade was made of lead and the gourd was filled with mercury. When the lead touched the mercury in the gourd, the blade disappeared. As for the Arhat image resembling the Buddhist elder, it was the statue that he had had remodeled before he left for home.

VI   *"Tower of Collected Elegance"*

"Tower of Collected Elegance" is an ugly story of a young man's loss of innocence, his initiation into evil, and his eventual revenge. It emphasizes the unlimited power wielded by those who rule and the total absence of power of the ruled. Perhaps in no other story by Li Yü is the contest between good and evil as sharply drawn as in this one.

The story centers on the tragic lives of three humble shopkeepers: Chin, Liu, and Ch'üan. Sharing many common interests and wishing to find occupations suited to their backgrounds, they select traditionally elegant goods in which to trade. After renting three adjoining shop-fronts, they open a bookstore, an incense store, and a florist and antique shop. Their happiness and success seem assured. Due to their diligence and intelligence, they soon have the rarest of books, plants, sandalwood, and antiques.

But misfortune soon visits them. When a notorious court official, Yen Shih-fan, hears about the handsomeness of Ch'üan, the youngest of the three shopkeepers, he pays them a visit and demands that Ch'üan serve him refreshments. Chin and Liu, suspicious of Yen's motives, send an elderly servant instead. Although displeased with his treatment, Yen hides his disappointment and buys all the items shown to him.

When, several days later, Chin and Liu present their bill, amounting to a thousand ounces of silver, they receive evasive answers from Yen's servants. Innocent of Yen's true intentions, they press for payment until one of Yen's servants tells them that his master wants Ch'üan. After a lengthy discussion, they decide to forfeit the money rather than sacrifice their young friend. When they inform Yen's servant of their decision, he warns them of what would happen if they offended a powerful court official—the complete ruin of their business and their persecution by Yen and his cronies.

Following another heated argument among the three shopkeepers, Ch'üan reluctantly agrees to see Yen. Ch'üan spends three days and nights at Yen's residence but stubbornly resists Yen's repeated attempts to seduce him. Outraged, Yen sacrifices Ch'üan to Eunuch Sha who first drugs the young man and then mercilessly castrates him. After the castration, Sha gives Ch'üan a few days leave to recuperate, making Chin and Liu pledge their own lives as guarantees for Ch'üan's return.

In telling this ugly tale, Li Yü emphasizes the helplessness of the lower classes, for in any confrontation with the rich and the powerful, justice is nonexistent. For even though Ch'üan's wrongs are revenged by the emperor later in the story, he has forever lost his manhood and innocence.

VII *"Tower of Rolling Clouds"*

In Yüan Chen's "The Story of Ying-ying," a T'ang dynasty short story which later inspired the writing of the dramatic play *The Western Chamber* (*Hsi-hsiang chi*), there is a clever maidservant. In the role of a go-between, she is instrumental in bringing her mistress Ying-ying and Scholar Chang together. In Li Yü's "Tower of Rolling Clouds," the maidservant, Neng Hung, matches her historical counterpart in cleverness: she not only brings her mistress and a scholar together but marries the scholar herself as well. How she achieves all that is, of course, what forms the dramatic interest in the story.

P'ei Ch'i-lang, married to an ugly wife, is treated to the view of two beautiful girls on an outing on the day of the Dragon Boat

Festival. He learns that they are Miss Wei, sixteen years of age, and her maid, Neng Hung, who is eighteen. Soon his ugly wife dies, after having caused him endless moments of anguish and embarrassment because of her ugliness and affectations. Determined to marry one or both of the beautiful girls, he seeks help from a matchmaker. But the matchmaker is soundly rebuffed by the Weis who resent that Ch'i-lang had previously reneged on his engagement to Miss Wei in order to marry a girl from a wealthy family. In traditional China, the groom usually had no idea what his prospective bride looked like; and Ch'i-lang had had no inkling of Miss Wei's attractiveness nor of the other girl's ugliness. Otherwise he would never have consented to give up Miss Wei regardless of the other's wealth. Being told that he has no chance with Miss Wei whatsoever, he falls on his knees and begs the matchmaker to arrange for him to marry the maid Neng Hung instead, a request that is impossible to fulfill. But watching his every move from a tower called "Rolling Clouds" located next door to the matchmaker's house, Neng Hung is impressed by Ch'i-lang's sincerity and works out an arrangement with him stipulating that if he will make her his second wife, she, in return, will help him get Miss Wei.

Soon the Weis decide to ask an astrologer to choose a suitable mate for their daughter, and Neng Hung bribes one nicknamed Iron-mouthed Chang to pick the horoscope of P'ei Ch'i-lang. Among the horoscopes given him to examine, Iron-mouthed Chang pretends to be surprised at finding Ch'i-lang's. Mr. Wei asks why. Chang replies that Ch'i-lang is destined to become a high government official, and that many families with eligible daughters have wanted him to be their son-in-law. Then Wei explains the situation and asks if Ch'i-lang's horoscope matches his daughter's. Faking a serious expression, Chang explains somberly that the two horoscopes do match, but that Mr. Wei must hurry because the lucky star his daughter is then under will leave her in three days. The matter is settled. The Weis will have Ch'i-lang as their son-in-law. On the wedding night, while Ch'i-lang goes through the wedding formalities with Miss Wei he actually spends the night with Neng Hung, without Miss Wei's knowing it, of course.

To carry out her plan, Neng Hung, soon after the marriage of Miss Wei to Ch'i-lang, reminds the Weis that her young mistress's horoscope only entitles her to half a husband and that her mistress must share him with someone else, otherwise disaster will follow.

The ending is a foregone conclusion. With seeming reluctance and after much urging from the others including Miss Wei, Neng Hung finally agrees to become Ch'i-lang's second wife.

The plot seems preposterous. The success of Neng Hung's schemes depends entirely on the gullibility of the Weis and the utter ignorance and stupidity of Miss Wei. Preposterous as it may seem, the Chinese were slaves to their superstitious beliefs, and in matters of betrothal an astrologer's words were usually treated seriously, particularly if the words came from someone with Iron-mouthed Chang's "reputation." Moreover, comic plots are usually absurd. For instance, if Scapin were not such a successful fraud, and if Signors Argante and Géronte were a little less stupid, Molière's comedy Les Fourberies de Scapin would not have been possible.[18]

VIII   "Tower of Ten Nuptial Winecups"

This story calls to mind the medieval form, the fabliau, a short comic or satiric tale in verse form dealing with middle- or lower-class characters and delighting in the ribald and the obscene. Li writes that a young man named Yao Tzu-ku is engaged to marry a Miss T'u. To insure their happiness, his father invites a clairvoyant to ask the gods to provide a name for one of the three buildings which have been erected especially for the wedding. After much drinking, the clairvoyant writes three characters: "Shih-chin lou" or "Tower of Ten Nuptial Winecups," the meaning of which baffles everyone. (The practice of invoking the divine to choose names for buildings was quite popular in premodern China.)

Soon Yao marries the beautiful Miss T'u. But on the wedding night, he discovers a mystery both unexpected and extraordinary. A ditty describes that moment of discovery:

> O Promise of Joy, what strangeness has befallen!
> I've had only a glimpse of Mount Wu
> And the way is lost;
> Where is the great vantage point
> Where I can hold commune with the clouds?
> The dual peaks are prominent,
> But the jade ravine, alas, is wanting. . . .[19]

Embracing his bride in great sorrow, he wonders why a beauty could be marred by such a monumental defect.

After apprising his parents of his bride's lack he resigns himself to fate. However, his parents secretly and immediately arrange with Miss T'u's parents for one of her sisters to replace her. On the night of the substitution, Yao returns home late and instantly falls asleep. Li Yü then reveals the bridegroom's second frustration. Her skin as coarse as leather, his new bride is not only ugly but also urinates in bed when asleep. Upon discovering this, Yao rushes to his parents demanding that his first wife be returned.

His parents discover that the first bride meanwhile has married someone else and consequently arrange to have the first bride's third sister as a second replacement. These two sisters—his first and third wives—look very much alike and the parents again fail to inform their son of the replacement. Yao is unable to tell the difference until he gets in bed with her. Then he finds that unlike the other two girls, his latest bride is a veteran bedmate; in fact, she is already five months pregnant. She is, of course, also returned to her parents.

After these unpleasant experiences, Yao marries again and again. One after another, the women are either too ugly or too stupid. One of them, a rich man's concubine, is snatched away from him at the last moment because the rich man's family has changed its mind about selling her to him. Within three short years, he has married nine times.

The tenth attempt brings different results. Through the efforts of his maternal uncle, Yao gets his tenth bride. After a brief wedding ceremony, he discovers that this last wife is actually his first. Because of her defect, she had been sold from one man to another and eventually found by Yao's uncle who was away from home on business. Yao is both happy and sad, for he loves her despite her defect. Their nightly embraces continue and soon sufficiently arouse her passion to activate a physical change in her anatomy. To everyone's surprise, she becomes a normal woman and is able to respond to him and make him feel truly like a man.

Mrs. Yao's case may seem unusual to the Western reader. Sun K'ai-ti, however, pointed out that during the Middle Ch'ing period, much later than Li Yü's time, a case was actually recorded that was allegedly similar to that described in "Tower of Ten Nuptial Winecups." The record reads as follows:

When Official Kao, a native of Kuangchou County, served in Anhui province, he took a concubine, because he was heirless. As she turned out to be a "stone girl," he returned her to her family. Later Official Kao moved to the eastern part of Kwangtung province and asked friends to find him a concubine. Strangely, the girl they chose was none other than his first concubine. She had had five husbands already. Moved, Kao said: "Fate decides that I not have any heir. What more can I say? This girl has a congenital defect, and if I throw her out, she will most surely have a tragic life. It's best that I keep her." Soon the girl's private parts swelled and a lump developed which rotted and burst open a gate. . . . Later she had a son. . . . She was very beautiful and her story was known throughout several provinces.[20]

Li Yü, of course, could not have known about the case of Official Kao and his concubine, and yet the manner in which the recorded account matches Li Yü's story testifies to Li's creative powers as a storyteller.

IX   "Tower of the Returning Crane"

This story presents and contrasts the fortunes of two young men: Yü and Tuan. Both are brilliant scholastically as well as good-looking. But that is where the resemblance ends. Yü clearly lacks a sense of moderation and is primarily interested in an unrestrained and unthinking pursuit of immediate sensual pleasures. A Chinese hedonist, he views marriage as one of man's basic pleasurable experiences and refuses to delay that experience. As soon as possible he marries Pearl, a great beauty. Vowing that he will never love another, he spends every possible moment with her. And when assigned to escort the tribute being sent to the Tartars by the emperor, he is emotionally and mentally unprepared for their separation. His pillow wet with tears, he says farewell to her over and over again, hoping for an early return. As the moment of parting arrives, he studies her face again and again. Even when seated on his horse, he keeps looking back so as to retain a vivid memory of her. Engulfed by her husband's engrossing love for her, Pearl finds the separation from him unbearable and soon dies of a broken heart.

Tuan's view of life is different. He believes with the Cynics that "The good life can be found only as man rids himself of all slavery to desire, of all bondage to external circumstances beyond his control."[21] Even though he passes his first degree examination at nine and is ready for the second degree examination at nineteen, he refuses to take the latter, feeling that if he passes it, he would immediately become a high official without having tasted the hardships of life. To avoid being spoiled by good fortune, he chooses to wait a few years to give himself time to mature.

Through the mysterious workings of fate, he marries Pearl's sister, Jade, who is even more beautiful than Pearl. But instead of basking in happiness, he has serious misgivings about his good fortune. Feeling unworthy and anticipating catastrophe, he is worried and fearful and tells his wife that everyone is entitled to only a limited amount of happiness and should, therefore, be sparing in using his alloted quota, and be prepared for difficult times. He fails to impress Jade with his wisdom and remains much of an enigma to her.

Like Yü, he, too, is assigned to escort tribute sent to the Tartars; but unlike Yü, he tells his wife she should consider his trip as an eternal parting. When his wife prepares clothes and shoes for him to take along, he unfeelingly insists that he will have no need for them and asks her to save them for someone else. Incensed by his insulting remarks, she burns all the clothing and shoes. He just watches the fire and makes no attempt to stop her. When the departure date comes, he packs his old clothes and leaves behind whatever new clothing was not consumed by the flames. Finally, he writes "Ho-kuei lou" or "Tower of the Returning Crane" on a tablet and fastens it on their house, indicating that he will never return alive.[22] When the moment of parting arrives, he behaves as if he were going on a short business trip and displays no emotion whatsoever, despite his wife's uncontrollable grief.

Once in the hands of the Tartars, he puts his theory of "accepting the worst" into practice. When tortured, his pain is relieved by his imagining even more painful punishment; he concludes that worldly punishments are preferable to those administered in Hell, and that the worst that can actually happen to him will be a death which he does not fear. No amount of torture can change his belief that there is nothing for him to do except to endure life patiently. His patience matches that of Epictetus (55–135 A.D.). When a slave in the household of a dissolute Roman, Epictetus used the Stoic philosophy to meet all unexpected situations. When his master had Epictetus's leg twisted, Epictetus pointed out that his leg would break, and when it did break, he said to his master unemotionally: "You see, it is as I told you."[23]

Tuan endures. After many years of terrible suffering, he is released by the Tartars and returns home feeling he has had his full share of privation. Now, a stoic-turned-hedonist, he wears a smile on his face and asks how his wife has enjoyed herself during their separation. Jade turns her face away and refuses to answer him. Pretending not to understand his wife's anger, he says: "It seems you haven't forgotten your grievances of the past, and you want me to apologize to you before you will speak to me. It is not that I'm bragging. I am truly the most affectionate husband in the world, and there is no one else like me. If anything, you should thank me and yet you want me to apologize to you."[24]

Angrily, she demands to know his reasons. He lists them as follows:

After eight years of separation, you haven't lost one ounce of weight but have gained handsomely. This is reason number one. You are eight years older, yet you haven't aged a bit but look even younger. This is reason number two. Your sister, Pearl, is dead, yet you are living and well. Whom should you thank? This is reason number three. Pearl's husband looks aged, yet I am just as youthful as ever. . . . This is reason number four. Yü and Pearl thought their parting temporary, and we thought ours eternal. Who could have known that their separation was to be eternal, and ours, only temporary? . . . This is reason number five. . . .[25]

Jade remains unconvinced, thinking he is "sweet-talking" her to cover up his previous indifference. To dispel her doubts, he asks her if she remembers having received a charm from him eight years ago. She takes out the charm on which is engraved a verse the meaning of which she never understood. He explains that it is a palindrome verse that can be read forward and backward. He asks her to read it backward and, miraculously, it is a love letter. Convinced of his love for her, she smiles gratefully.

Tuan becomes a different person. No longer morose, he jubilantly celebrates their reunion. He orders wedding candles bought, lanterns lighted, and music by professional bands played. That same evening he behaves like a carefree bridegroom. He knows he has had his share of misfortune and now can begin to enjoy life.

X *"Tower of Ancestral Worship"*

In seventeenth-century China, a man was allowed to take concubines and divorce his wives, while a woman was expected to follow the dictum of the three obediences and the four virtues. Her three obediences were to obey her father before marriage, her husband after marriage, and her son after the death of her husband; and her four virtues were womanly attainments, speech, appearance, and skills. In fact, she was told to emulate the virtuous women in Liu Hsiang's *Biographies of Illustrious Women (Lieh-nü chuan)*. A virtuous woman, it is said, would rather end her life than break the rules of proper conduct or *li*. One anecdote in the *Biographies of Illustrious Women* tells how Heroine Meng Chi attempted suicide when confronted with the necessity of riding in an open carriage that would improperly expose her, and an encomium in the book praises her for adhering to the rules of *li*; other anecdotes describe the deeds of women who sacrifice their lives to save either their husbands or their fathers; still others demonstrate that the most praiseworthy virtue is chastity.[26] To ensure her chastity, a woman should be ready to commit suicide upon the death of her fiancé or husband, and thus be canonized as the ideal of female abnegation.[27]

In "Tower of Ancestral Worship" Li Yü deals with a woman's fulfillment of her obligations to her husband and consequently to her society. Instead of describing her in terms of abstract virtues, he vividly highlights her internal conflicts and thus makes her realistic.

During the last years of the Ming dynasty, Li narrates, there lived near Nanking a scholar named Shu, the only heir in a family which had never had more than one son during each of the last seven generations. After several years of marriage, his wife has a son. This is a period of civil disorder and the threat of outlaws is such that nine out of ten pregnant women abort their unborn to spare them the suffering that would ensue were they to fall into the hands of these outlaws. Up until then Shu has never seriously considered the threat of the outlaws. He becomes so worried that he shares his apprehensions with his wife and expresses the wish that she protect their son at all costs. Mrs. Shu, however, demurs, arguing that a woman's reputation depends on her virtue, that is, on the preservation of her chastity. Their conversation ends inconclusively. Soon the outlaws near the city walls and Shu reminds his wife of her duty to preserve the life of the baby so that there will be someone to carry on his family's name. She insists that this is a matter on which her elder clansmen must be consulted.

Shu invites them to gather at the family temple and solicits their opinions. They unanimously agree that it is more important for Mrs. Shu to save the baby than to remain virtuous, and ask her to accept their decision. Still unwilling, she argues that the baby is very young and has not even had such childhood diseases as measles and smallpox; if she should sacrifice her name and he should die anyhow, she would then have sacrificed everything in vain. The clansmen reply that her job is to do her best and not worry about how long the child is destined to live. Still looking for a way out, she maintains that prayers should be made to the ancestors and their guidance sought.

Her suggestion is approved and the clansmen advise Shu to write the characters for "preserving the virtue" and "preserving the heir" on two separate pieces of paper which are then rolled up into balls. After paying respect to the ancestors, Mrs. Shu picks one of the two balls—the one on which is written "preserving the heir." The clansmen and Shu are delighted with the outcome. Mrs. Shu finally gives in and, after paying obeisance to the ancestors four times, vows: "I shall never talk about 'virtue' any more in this life; and I pray that peace come to the earth soon."[28] Sadly, she takes the baby and goes home with her husband.

The outlaws capture the city in two weeks. Shu barely escapes. When the outlaws approach Mrs. Shu, she holds the baby tightly in her arms and won't let him go despite threats of violence, determined to surrender her body only if they leave the baby unharmed. Awed by her fierce determination, they comply with her wish and take her and the baby to another city.

When Shu returns following the departure of the outlaws, he finds no trace of his wife or baby. He wanders for years throughout the country looking for them. Robbed and stripped of his belongings by bandits on the road, and later made into a boat-tracker during the day and locked up at night by government soldiers, he cries every night. Eventually, his crying attracts the attention of a general's wife in a boat anchored not too far from the shore. She orders Shu be brought before her. Separated from him by a curtain, she listens to his tale, and then, without explanation, orders him to be chained securely until her husband's return. On the fourth day, the general returns from his mission in Szechwan. He wonders why Shu has been crying, interrogates him, and examines his wounds. With apparent satisfaction, he comments that had it not been for the chain and the wound it made on Shu's neck, he would have killed him — and for nothing. Married to the former Mrs. Shu, the general, a suspicious man by nature, had wanted to see the wound to prove that no improprieties had taken place between Shu and his wife during his absence. Satisfied with his wife's loyalty to him, he magnanimously returns the child to Shu and asks Shu to leave.

Meanwhile, Mrs. Shu, thinking that she has fulfilled her promise to the Shu family, attempts to take her own life. Saved in time by the general, she is returned to Shu who has not yet traveled a great distance.

Obedient to her husband and her clansmen to whom she has fulfilled her promise, and having attempted to preserve her honor by taking her own life after the child was returned to her husband, Mrs. Shu is a perfect woman by conventional Confucian standards. By detailing her inner conflicts, it is obvious that Li Yü's sympathy lies with her. In her initial questions to her husband and clansmen, she challenges the right of society to make such severe demands on a woman, whom that society believed was physically and mentally inferior to her male counterpart. And, not just incidentally, Mrs. Shu is the one in the story on whom all the responsibilities fall.

XI *"Tower of My Birth"*

Kenneth Latourette in *The Chinese, Their History and Culture* points out that "sons were so indispensable in carrying on the family line and in maintaining the honors to ancestors that failure to have them was regarded as a serious offense against filial piety. Without sons the rites to parents could not be continued, and not only would the living be disgraced, but the spirits of the dead, deprived of such service, would be in misery."[29] Indeed, continuation of the family line was a major concern to people of all social classes. Confucius said most unequivocally that the greatest of the three filial impieties was not to have a male heir, which was a major theme in the preceding story, "Tower of Ancestral Worship."

The present story deals with the last years of the Sung dynasty and a thrifty millionaire named Yin Hou who lived in the province of Hupeh. After years of marriage, his wife gives birth to a son, who, though impressive in appearance and size, has only a single testicle. The Yins are concerned that he is sterile but are reasonably contented that the family line can be continued for at least one more generation. When the son is three or four, he disappears and it is rumored that he might have been eaten by a wild animal. Overwhelmed by grief, the Yins gradually adapt to their new situation and in time decide to adopt a son, but from a far away place since their friends and relatives know they are wealthy and might want to exploit them by showering false affections upon them in the hope of being adopted.

His clothes old, torn, and patched and disguised as an old vagabond, Yin attaches a twisted ring of straw to his hat, signifying that he is for sale. To curious onlookers he explains that he wants a wealthy man to buy him as his father. On a sheet of paper he writes the following lines:

> Old and without a son,
> I sell myself as someone's father.
> I ask for only ten ounces of silver;
> If interested, cash on delivery and
> No further regrets.[30]

Wherever he goes he carries this sign. When tired of walking, he sits cross-legged hanging the sign on his chest in the manner of a Buddhist monk soliciting alms. From bystanders everywhere he receives almost the same reactions: some curse him, some jeer him, and some consider him insane. But he remains composed and undisturbed, continuing his search for a buyer.

When a young man named Yao indicates interest, Yin spells out his harsh conditions: that he is spoiled, that he needs money to buy particularly good food and wine from time to time, and so on. But the young man seems undeterred and is determined to finalize the agreement, even complimenting Yin for his thoughtfulness. After the transaction, Yao says to Yin: "Dear father, here are six ounces more than your sales price. From now on, you are in charge of all money matters. Eat and drink as you please. As long as I can afford it, you shall have the very best."[31] From then on, old Yin and young Yao live together happily. Whatever Yin wants, Yao supplies with pleasure. At times Yin tests Yao's patience by refusing to eat delicacies especially purchased for him, but the young man remains patient and affectionate.

Soon the area is threatened by outlaws. Yin reveals his identity to Yao and invites Yao to go home with him. Yao in turn informs his adopted father that he would like to have his fiancée, a Miss Ts'ao, with him and goes to look for her by himself. It turns out that Miss Ts'ao has been kidnapped by outlaws who are nearby, and are auctioning off women tied in sacks that cover them completely. Yao picks one at random and it has an old woman in it. At first a little surprised and disappointed, Yao asks the old woman to be his adopted mother since he has never known his own mother. Moved by Yao's sincerity and love, she instructs him to go back to the auction next day to find the sack in which there is a beautiful girl from a good family, and says that he can identify the sack by feeling it since the girl always carries a measuring stick with her. Of course, the girl is none other than Miss Ts'ao, and the stick the one that Yao had given her as a token of love. Li explains that Yao gave her such a present because the latter is a cloth merchant.

At this point in the story, Yao realizes that his adopted father has forgotten to give him his real address, and reluctantly accepts the old woman's invitation to go home with her. Together the three of them journey to the old woman's home. Still more coincidences are to come. For one, it turns out that the old woman is actually Mrs. Yin. She was kidnapped soon after her husband left home by the same outlaws who kidnapped Miss Ts'ao.

After everyone has been happily reunited, one more miracle occurs. Once settled in the Yins' house, Yao seems to remember having seen everything there. He remembers the shutters, the windows, the furniture, and even recalls a box of toys in one of the rooms. To solve the puzzle, Mr. Yin takes Yao aside and examines the latter's private parts. Afterward he ecstatically declares that Providence has brought them back together. This denouement has similarities in Western literature, as in Shakespeare, for instance, when Cesario reveals to the duke in *Twelfth Night* that he is really Viola, and in Fielding when the reader learns that Joseph Andrews is in reality the true issue of Mr. and Mrs. Wilson.

The happy ending reaffirms the traditional Chinese belief that virtuous men will always be rewarded by Providence. In this case, Providence arranged for old Mrs. Yin and young Miss Ts'ao to be kidnapped by the same outlaws and thrown together in the same place. If the outlaws had decided to sell the young woman first, the Yins would probably have had a much more difficult time in being reunited. And if Mrs. Yin had been bought by another man, Yao and Miss Ts'ao might never have met and their reunion never have occurred. Of course, the possibilities are infinite.

From a Chinese point of view, old Mr. Yin's tireless efforts to find a worthy son as a way to discharge his obligations to his ancestors are praiseworthy; and young Yao seems to typify the virtues of filial piety and benevolence. His innate desire first to buy a father and

later to buy a mother betrays his subconscious wish to fulfill the
obligations of filial piety. This wish, in turn, reflects itself in his
benevolent deeds, and particularly in his treatment of old Mrs. Yin.
Due to his clear manifestation of the two cardinal virtues of filial
piety and benevolence, he, again, from the Chinese point of view,
deserves whatever blessings he has received or will be receiving. In
fact, Li Yü tells the reader that despite Yao's single testicle, he
fathers many children and the family will thus continue to prosper
for many generations.

XII   *"Tower of Heeding Criticism"*

During the years between the collapse of the Ming regime and
the establishment of the Ch'ing, Li withdrew to the countryside and
wrote a number of idyllic verses, one of which introduces the present story.[32] The story is concerned with the recluse, a popular
theme in Chinese literature as documented by Nemoto Makoto in
*The Spirit of Resistance in Authoritarian Society (Sensei shakai ni
okeru teiko seishin).*[33] Makoto gives numerous examples of men who
renounced the official life and withdrew into the countryside.

In "Tower of Heeding Criticism," Li describes a resilient man
named Ku Ai-sou. After failing his second-degree examinations several times, he completely abandons an academic career at the age of
thirty. Soon he discards his first-degree regalia, and burns all his
books except those related to farming. He then purchases a few
acres of land outside the city limits and vows never to return to the
city. His unannounced departure from the city deeply disturbs his
friends who immediately urge him to return. Succumbing to their
repeated pleas, he returns and resettles on a piece of land containing a few huts, just outside the city limits. What makes Ku admirable, in Li Yü's view, is Ku's willingness to compromise his principles
with the realities of life. Thus Ku is true to himself and yet satisfies
the demands of his friends as well. In short, what Ku exemplifies is
the Confucian ideal of the Golden Mean (*chung-yung*), which is "to
be central (*chung*) [in our moral being] and to be harmonious (*yung*)
[with all],"[34] or simply not to take extreme positions in anything.

But even if Ku represents the supreme man who exemplifies the
principle of the Golden Mean, Yin, his cousin, is equally admirable.
Upon hearing of Ku's departure from the city, he is saddened by the
loss of the one who was teaching him morals. Remembering that Ku
had given him moral instructions in one particular room of his

house, he renames it "Tower of Heeding Criticism," and gets Ku's other friends to arrange for Ku's return to the city. After Ku has settled in the cottage outside the city limits, he buys the piece of property next to Ku so that his friend is always available to give him advice. In concluding this story, Li explains why both Ku and Yin are admirable. He feels that in this world people like Ku are rare, but rarer still are ones like Yin who accept criticism with a willing heart and an open mind, and that the existence of ones like Ku and Yin, few as they are, should be made widely known.

Sun K'ai-ti considers the story autobiographical. The similarities between Li Yü and Ku are such that the picture of Ku could very well be Li's own portrait.[35] Ku's failure to pass his second-degree examinations corresponds with Li Yü's own situation, and Ku's retreat into the countryside reflects Li's frequently expressed wish to get away from his own despised way of earning a livelihood: begging money from his patrons. And lastly, Cousin Yin's friendship with Ku is what Li would want of his many friends.

CHAPTER 4.

Li's Achievement as Storyteller

I *Conventions and Structure*

A S stated in Chapter 2, fiction writing was a direct descendant of
oral storytelling on street corners and in places of public
gathering and entertainment. To sustain the interest of early arrivals, storytellers recited one or two poems or told a minitale before
narrating the main story. Consequently, a traditional Chinese story
usually consists of an introduction, the story proper, and a moralistic
epilogue. The introduction consists of a chapter title in couplet
form, a verse poem or two, followed by a minitale or comments
related to the main story. To advance the narration, there are the
presence of the narrator, frequent recapitulations of the plot, and an
ample supply of verse quotations spread throughout the story.[1]

Li Yü follows that narrative tradition. Except for a few stories,
they all begin with a standard chapter title in couplet form, a poem
or two, a minitale or random remarks on subjects related to the
story, and conclude with a moralistic epilogue.

His chapter titles usually give a hint of the action to come. For
example, the first chapter of "Tower of Collected Elegance" begins
with the following chapter title: "The Florist Refuses to Sell the
Blossom of His Rear Courtyard;/ The Buyer is Used to Purchasing a
Priceless Commodity."[2] At first glance, the meaning of the title is
unclear, and yet the title is so cleverly phrased that it intrigues the
reader to want to know what it means. Thus, the title provides a
preview of what will happen and also how it will happen. It is only
after the reader has read the complete chapter that he will be able to
understand the title's full meaning: "The Florist" refers to Ch'üan,
the victim, who is a florist by trade; "The Blossom of His Rear
Courtyard" refers to the homosexual activities demanded of him;
"The Buyer" refers to Yen Shih-fan, a powerful court official, who is
used to purchasing "a Priceless Commodity," an allusion to his get-

78

ting homosexual favors from others. Since no one can "price" homosexual favors, such favors are consequently referred to as "a Priceless Commodity."

In general, Li's introductory minitales offer humorous little incidents or crudely developed plot outlines to illustrate the themes of the main story. For instance, in "A Handsome Man, Trying to Avoid Sex Scandals, Manages to Create Them," he starts with the minitale of a rice merchant arguing with a sugar merchant over the ownership of a measuring basket. Unable to settle the squabble between themselves, they take their dispute to a judge. By treating the basket as if it were a person, the judge interrogates it thoroughly but fails to receive any answers. Outraged, he orders it to be flogged severely. The flogging does bring results. For after seeing some sesame seeds lying on the ground, the judge concludes that the basket must have belonged to the sugar merchant, sesame seeds not being sold in a rice merchant's shop.

In "Tower of Rolling Clouds," Li alerts masters to the tricks of maidservants, who move freely in and out of the women's quarters, and who often try to make themselves popular by sacrificing their mistresses' good reputations. With such a theme in mind, he narrates a minitale:

During the Ming dynasty, a virtuous woman lost her husband at eighteen and remained a widow until she was in her forties. Neither her clansmen nor her parents could make her change her mind. Her heart was truly as firm as iron, and she had accomplished many things. Then suddenly one night she was raped in her sleep. In her state of semiconsciousness, she felt a man's body on top of her. . . . When it was all over, she suddenly woke up, realizing that the man was a stranger, and she herself a widow. She asked him how he got in and so on.

The stranger, confident that nothing drastic would happen to him, told her the truth. It turned out that the widow's maid had had an illicit relationship with the man for a long time. Afraid that her affair would be discovered by her mistress, she persuaded him to involve her mistress as well. . . .

After the man had left, the widow mused that her virtuous reputation of more than twenty years' standing had been ruined by the maid. What was she to do? She could neither forget the rape nor speak of it to others. She finally decided to summon the maid before her, and she bit her several times. After heaving a few long sighs, she hanged herself. Later her family members discovered the truth and brought the case before a judge who sentenced both the man and the maid to death.[3]

If the widow's story is an effective introduction to the main story, then the introductory tale to "Tower of the Returning Crane" provides philosophical insight into life. During the middle of summer, Li narrates, a wealthy traveler shares a hotel room with a poor man. Mosquitoes are everywhere and the wealthy man's mosquito net does not shut out their annoying hum. In utter misery, he thinks fondly of his sweet home where the maids fan him and chase the mosquitoes away. Meanwhile, the poor man jumps out of his netless cot and keeps moving around to fend off the mosquitoes. The rich man takes pity on his roommate who rejects both pity and sympathy and insists he is happy. Asked why he is happy, the poor man explains: "At first, I too complained about misery, but when I thought of something, I forgot my misery." Questioned further as to what he means by "something," he answers: "Of the miseries of those in jail, locked in their pillories. Even if they were bitten to death by the mosquitoes, they could not complain. How could they have the complete freedom I have? Therefore, even though my body has a hard life, my spirit does not suffer one bit. Unknowingly and unconsciously I feel pleased with myself."[4]

Li Yü then summarizes his views: "If all the poor people in the world used the same rationalization to see hell as heaven and adversity as prosperity, then one could play his lute under the *Huang-lien* [*Coptis japonica*, known for its bitter taste] tree and be joyous and happy living in a slum. No one would ever need to look prematurely old, and misery would disappear in time."[5]

A believer in the Buddhist concept of retribution, Li Yü metes out justice fairly and swiftly: the wicked are punished and the virtuous are rewarded either with rank or by having distinguished descendants who bring fame and honor to the family. A typical epilogue reads as follows: "In the course of their lives the father and the son both accumulated much virtue. And though the son had only one testicle, he fathered many generations of offspring who all had single testicles. . . . And the family remained prosperous until the *Hung-chih* years of the Ming dynasty [1488–1505]. . ."[6]

In short, although Li follows the traditional form of the short story, he is not without innovations. First, the narrator is less ubiquitous in his stories than are those in the *San-yen* and *Erh-p'o* collections. Phrases such as "Now I speak of . . . ," "My story takes two courses," "But I shall stop this chitchat" are very rare. Second, in place of frequent recapitulations of the plot, he allows his stories to develop by themselves. Third, with the exception of "Tower of Joining Reflections," verse quotations are usually confined to the introduction and are used sparingly. Fourth, he is unique in naming every story in *Twelve Towers* after a *lou;* this provides a measure of unity and coherence to the whole collection. Fifth, he is the first Ch'ing writer to vary the length of his stories. Some have one chapter and others three to six, a bold innovative step which differentiates them from the stories in the *San-yen* and *Erh-p'o* collections, each of which has one chapter.

II *The Language*

Apart from his innovations in narrative techniques, Li was a master of language. Although trained in the classics, he deliberately chose to write colloquially and in a straightforward fashion. The following excerpt from "By a Strange Bargain a Bodhisattva Transforms a Daughter Into a Son" shows Li at his colloquial best:

There was this rich man living by the seashore. Who did not flatter him? His wife and he enjoyed all kinds of happiness, but they had one regret. He was already close to sixty years of age, and yet had no male offspring. His wife, jealous by nature, had refused to allow him a concubine before she reached fifty, claiming that she could yet have a son by him. Who could know that she would not have even one "empty-hearted egg" by the time she reached seven times seven—forty-nine years of age. Having passed the change of life, she realized the hopelessness of her case and reluctantly agreed to let her husband have a few concubines. Though he did not indulge in sex wantonly, he did faithfully sow seeds in his concubines following their menstruation. It was most strange. Were these women with other men, they would have become pregnant if the men only caressed them a little without even going to the trouble of sleeping together. But once they entered his household, they became like castrated pigs or dogs. No matter what he did to them, even cohabiting with them sideways or in a standing position, they remained sterile. . . .[7]

A second example of Li's use of racy, supple, and vital language occurs when a man is speaking to his brother: "If you are afraid of being cheated by us [himself and another brother], why didn't you come into the world a little sooner? Instead you allowed us to squander all the money on whores. Now you are digging for farts in a dead man's asshole."[8]

Apart from employing earthy language, Li writes lucidly and simply in a lively, effortless style. The fluency of his prose matches that of many modern Chinese authors writing in the vernacular. For instance, he describes an intelligent young woman as follows:

Her appearance and manners, though graceful and elegant much resembling a fairy-goddess on earth, cannot be considered beautiful enough to upset states and cities. But her intelligence and quickness in learning can be considered unparalleled. During her early childhood she studied with her brothers and could read four or five lines when they could only manage one. While the teacher explained the meaning of one sentence, she could understand the meaning of ten others. When she was fifteen, an age unsuitable for her to study under a male tutor any longer, she was already better prepared than her instructor and had no more need of his instruction. She wrote a good script, and painted well. Because of her father's occasional interest in calligraphy and painting, she soon mastered both arts simply by watching him. . . .[9]

And Li combines suggestion with compression in his description of the two Ch'ien girls in "Tower of Matrimonial Contest":

Though it is a common belief that boys resemble their fathers in looks, and girls their mothers, these two resembled neither. They looked so different from their parents that observers often thought they were adopted. Exquisitely beautiful and intelligent, they were a sharp contrast to their repulsive-looking and slow-thinking parents. When they were a little over ten, they were already as beautiful as dewy-red cherry apples and became more charming with each passing day. When they reached fourteen, they were so charming that not only the young lost their souls upon seeing them but also the old who could not resist saying: "Too beautiful, too beautiful."[10]

Even though the specifics of their beauty are withheld, the description suggests Oriental Helens of Troy. If they could draw the attention of the old, their beauty must have been stunning, since interest in women and sex is supposed to decrease with age.

In another passage, Li uses the same suggestive technique to delineate two women walking in the rain:

Among the women were two teenage girls. They were so exotically charming that it dazzled the eyes to look at them. Their wet clothing partially revealed their well-built, soft, and seemingly boneless bodies, and even their jadelike breasts became half-visible. . . . In the rain, sharing one umbrella, the two girls sometimes walked so slowly that they just ambled—and ambling made them appear even more desirable. Then suddenly they would walk fast, so fast that the spectators felt sorry for them. Though they knew they were being observed in a situation not entirely proper for young ladies, they remained calm, graceful, and composed. . . .[11]

Moreover, Li adopts a variety of styles in his verse passages, ranging from the colloquial style of:

> You cut my balls off, I cut off your head.
> Fair exchange, the upper for the lower.
> Death you truly deserved.
> You played with my private parts,
> So I dirtied your mouth.
> Fair exchange, the clean for the dirty.
> Even in death you leave a nauseating smell.
> A word to the people of this world:
> Never be scheming and foully sly,
> For every evil deed brings its own retribution.[12]

to the formal style of:

> Emulate mountains and hills
> But never the polluted water flowing
>   downstream.
> Reaching the top of a mountain take a
>   backward glance.
> Water never flows backward.
> To stop waves use hills as embankment,
> Never use water as a boat to carry stones.
> Paint a scroll of mountain and water;
>   hang it on your wall.
> Allow it to help you to reform your morals.[13]

the descriptive style of:

> A face as dark as black lacquer,
> Skin as cracked as ice,
> A rare scar on her cheek,
> Very much like the tear mark of the two
>   Hsiang princesses.[14]
> Fingers like green jade,
> Teeth like black silver.
> Rolling her eyes,
> She scares you stiff![15]

the rhetorical style of:

> Is this Ho-yang district?
> I thought that it was Sui-chin neighborhood.
> Mere buds when they were bought.
> Now sold as flowers with lingering fragrance.
> Prices fluctuate as bees crowd one another
> And busy patrons chase the wings of butterflies.
> Descendants of princes, don't be stingy with cash.
> Springtime is what cannot be bought.[16]

the lyrical flow of:

> Cities and towns are dens for war horses;
> Allow me to live in the country.
> One wife and without too many children,
> Only one sack of books and my lute I shall take.
> Though the peach blossoms of Ch'in are distant,
> The flowing waters of Wu-lin smell sweet.[17]
> Go I shall and now
> And never glance backward to the battlefield.[18]

or the allusive style of:

> The Milky Way is shallow and clear.
> The Herd-boy and the Spinning-damsel stand
>   on opposite banks of the river of stars,
> Eagerly awaiting their yearly reunion.
> Tonight is the night of their rendezvous.
> . . . .
> Each loves and is loved, relishing and enjoying
>   every second of the fleeting night,
> Praying that dawn would never come.
> . . . .
> Haven't you, sir, also witnessed human
>   separation and eternal parting?
> . . . .
> A beauteous maid, once gone, will never return.[19]

Despite the variety of styles he uses in his poems, they essentially retain the fluency and ease of his prose. Even when he uses allusions, they are few and chosen with discrimination. His references to the district of Ho-yang, the Sui-chin neighborhood, and the Milky Way are all general allusions; they serve to compact or compress images while contrasting time and space, night and day. Referring to the legend of the Herb-boy and the Spinning-damsel in "Tower of the Returning Crane," he contrasts the mythical couple's yearly reunion with the eventual reunion of Tuan and Jade and the separation of Yü and Pearl, two pairs of ill-starred lovers. In brief, there is a definite correlation between his allusions and the content of his stories. In love stories, he alludes to legends, myths, and earlier literature; in stories of political and social conditions, he cites Confucian classics and official histories. Everywhere he uses allusions sparingly and wisely, avoiding displays of pomposity.

His prose style is colloquial, straightforward, lively, and suggestive, and his poetic styles range from the colloquial to the allusive. Committed to the principle of immediate comprehensibility, he never seeks merely to show erudition, and writes clear and vivid sentences, devoid of superfluous detail. Even though prudish critics might find fault with some of his vulgar or indecent descriptions, they are fully justifiable on the ground that vice and depravity can never be excluded in the work of a realist, who looks at life honestly.

III *Characterization*

E. M. Forster divides characters into flat and round. The first, also known as types or caricatures, are constructed around a single idea or quality; the second are complex in temperament and motivation and are represented with subtle particularity.[20] Under Forster's definition, almost all of Li's characters are flat and may be considered unsatisfactory by Western literary standards. For example, John L. Bishop voices his dissatisfaction with characterization in Chinese fiction in his article "Limitations of Chinese Fiction":

In the matter of character portrayal, another contrast between Chinese and Western fiction is apparent. Both literatures attempt realistic portrayals of social types and the difference between them is one of degree. Both exploit dialogue as a means of differentiating between character and caste. The novel of the West, however, explores more thoroughly the minds of characters, and long familiarity with this realm has made possible whole novels which are confined to the individual mind alone, such as those of Virginia Woolf and James Joyce. But to the Chinese novelist, the mental life of his fictional characters is an area to be entered only briefly when necessary and then with timidity. For this reason, his ability to exploit one of the chief concerns of realistic fiction, the discrepancy between appearance and reality, is severely limited since he can rarely show us the sharp variance between what is said and what is thought.[21]

Bishop's observations probably accurately reflect most Chinese fiction, since the deep probing of character has not been part of the art of the Chinese storyteller, who has always been more interested in presenting recognizable social and human types. In fact, type characters have always been a feature of Chinese history and literature. For example, in Ssu-ma Ch'ien's *Records of the Historian* (*Shih-chi*) we find biographies grouped under the following categories: "Confucian Scholars," "Knights-Errant," "Merchants," and "Assassins." Even in the *Biographies of Illustrious Women* by Liu Hsiang, we find a "gallery of portraits of women, with many of them sharing particular virtues or a certain range of habits, values, or emotions."[22] The Sung and Ming stories and oral narratives contain a repertoire of stock characters, all distinguished by type features such as devotion to government, filial piety, preservation of chastity and honor by women, and unselfish sacrifices of one's self for friends.

When the Chinese literary tradition concerning character portrayal has been taken into account, the reader is likely to be impressed by the relatively wide range of social types Li Yü presents in his twenty-four stories. They range from the lowest on the Chinese social scale (beggars, bandits, prostitutes, swindlers, matchmakers, *yamen* runners, pawnbrokers, and common tradesmen), to representatives of the middle and ruling classes (scholars, district magistrates, country squires, generals, high court officials, and even emperors). They exhibit types of characters or of professional conduct—the heartless prostitute, the clever swindler, the romantic scholar, the snobbish country squire, the corrupted official— such as were familiar in the literature of the age. And taken together, they cover nearly the whole range of life in seventeenth-century China.

Using an omniscient point of view, Li tells and shows in dramatic scenes the motives of his characters. Frequently, by individualizing a conventional type, he creates new and memorable figures. For instance, his descriptions of the lovers Yü and Tuan in "Tower of the

Returning Crane" and of the virtuous Mrs. Shu in "Tower of Ancestral Worship" are such that they remain in the reader's imagination long after the details of their adventures have been forgotten. In short, Li succeeds in breathing life into his characters and in convincing the reader of their reality.

IV *Plot*

Northrop Frye divides fiction into the myth, the romance, and the novel in his *Anatomy of Criticism;*[23] the plots in Li Yü's stories easily fit into Frye's classifications. Under the rubric of the myth (which deals with gods), Li writes of divine powers taking a jealous concubine from the bed of her husband and depositing her in a pigsty, a Bodhisattva transforming a baby girl into a baby boy, and the ghost of a father wreaking vengeance upon a gambling broker. Under the romance (which deals with heroes and heroines), Li describes the heroic exploits of the swindler in "Tower of Self-reformation," of Mrs. Shu in "Tower of Ancestral Worship," and of Mrs. Keng in "A Female Ch'en P'ing Plots Seven Schemes." And under the novel (which deals with ordinary humans), Li elaborates on the anguish of an ugly man seeking a woman not averse to his looks; the good fortune of a *yamen* runner after having had his horoscope changed; the revenge of a eunuch in using his enemy's head as a urinal; the eventual marital bliss of a bridegroom after ten attempts at marriage; and the auctioning of women captives in sacks. In short, Li Yü gives his reader what Frye calls just enough romance "to project his libido on the hero and his anima on the heroine" and just enough realism "to keep these projections in a familiar world."[24]

In nearly all his stories, Li has perfect control of the rising action, climax, and falling action. Giving his reader intriguing plots and sometimes dramatic surprises at the end, he keeps him in suspense wondering what will happen when the hero or heroine is faced with the next dilemma and must choose between two courses of actions, neither of which may be desirable. Mindful of artistic unity, Li seldom includes an incident or episode not central to the development of the story. Arranging his incidents chronologically, he always follows a logical progression from one episode to the next consistent with the relationship of cause and effect. Lastly, in offering his reader neat resolutions to impossible or improbable conflicts, Li satisfies the reader's curiosity while simultaneously amusing him.

V *Theme*

Li Yü uses love as the theme in a great many stories. Even though nearly all his male lovers are handsome and his females beautiful, he gives less emphasis to the traditional exchange of love letters or to demonstrations of the male or female lover's erudition than one finds in a typical story like "Miss Su Thrice Quizzes the Bridegroom" (*Su Hsiao-mei san nan hsin-lang*), which is included in the *Stories to Warn Men* (*Hsing-shih Heng-yen*). Instead, he emphasizes physical fulfillment.[25] In "Tower of Joining Reflections," he stresses the delights of Chen-sheng and Yü-chüan upon first discovering their reflections in the water, their face-to-face meeting, their frustrations resulting from parental interference, and their eventual marriage. In "Tower of the Returning Crane," he dwells on the physical anguish of parting between newlyweds, on Yü and Pearl's eternal separation, and the ecstasy of Tuan and Jade's eventual reunion. And in "Tower of Ten Nuptial Winecups," he singles out the frustration of the nonconsummation of love, and of the pleasure in its eventual fulfillment. A liberal at heart, he mocks and scorns parental carelessness and thoughtlessness in arranging marriages for their children and heartily endorses the right of the children to choose the mates they consider ideal in such stories as "Tower of Matrimonial Contest" and "Tower of Rolling Clouds."

Writing about a recluse in "Tower of Heeding Criticism," he points out both the attractiveness of the ideal of withdrawing from society and its practical difficulties; in his stories about the Confucian themes of loyalty, filial piety, chastity, and righteousness, he makes clear the sacrifices involved in fulfilling one's obligations to the throne, to parents, to husbands, and to friends, and he openly wonders whether they are justified. And lastly, he emphasizes the grave importance of justice by presenting examples of social injustice and the need for them to be corrected by the authorities.

Li Yü feels deeply that he has an obligation to act as a moral guardian of society. He seeks to make the cowardly brave, the lustful pure, the miserly generous, and the dullard ashamed.[26] By putting men and women in different situations, Li shows their human failings and strengths. He mercilessly attacks the jealous, the snobbish, the greedy, the lecherous; he pities the ignorant and the gullible; and he admires the loyal, the faithful, and the righteous. Putting man in his social context, he exposes the evils of established seventeenth-century customs, including the practice of consulting an astrologer in matters of betrothal, employing matchmakers in arranged marriages, the denial of rights to concubines and bondservants, the demands made on women, the excessive emphasis placed on having a male heir, the privileges of the upper classes, and the inequities inherent in the contemporary social system. Primarily a bourgeois at heart, he envisages no radical changes in social and political situations and satisfies himself by drawing the public's attention to important social issues.

VI *Conclusion*

Comparing *Drama Without Sound* to *Twelve Towers*, we find the latter to have been written by a more sophisticated storyteller. In the latter stories, for example, we find standardized three-character titles, more elaborate introductory poems and minitales which better reflect the content of each story and provide better introductions to the main stories, a less obtrusive presence of the narrator, dialogue used more extensively, more developed and complex plots with fewer instances of divine intervention, a greater variety of characters, ones whose psyches are more subtly probed, and a greater concern with vital social issues. From the viewpoint of narrative techniques, *Twelve Towers* is also superior to *Drama Without Sound*, and this is not to denigrate the importance of *Drama Without Sound* to the development of Li Yü as a storyteller. Without the experience he received in the writing of *Drama Without Sound*, it is doubtful if Li could have achieved the level of sophistication he demonstrated in *Twelve Towers*. Perhaps it would not be too far off the mark to say that *Drama Without Sound*, with its warts and blemishes, is the work of an apprentice-writer, and *Twelve Towers* solid testimony to the successful completion of that apprenticeship.

In sum, Li Yü wrote about imperial China, and his achievement lies in vividly portraying the period and its people in his stories. Not only are the plots interesting, the people realistic, and the period intriguing, but the stories are also morally instructive, fitting Robert Frost's definition of a good poem—from delight to wisdom. The experience of reading Li's stories is exactly that: delightful and instructive.

CHAPTER 5

Prayer Mat of Flesh (Jou p'u-t'uan)

I *Authorship*

THOUGH *Hui-wen chuan* (*The Palindromic Affair*), a long novel in sixteen *chüan*, has been attributed to Li Yü, most critics believe that it probably was not authored by him because of its inferior quality.[1] On the other hand, *Prayer Mat of Flesh* has generally been considered one of his works. Pornographic in content, it centers on the amorous adventures of a young scholar and his eventual moral redemption. First published in 1633, it has never been widely available in China, the governments of which have maintained a rigidly puritanical, Neo-Confucianistic, and hypocritical stance since the early Ch'ing period. Outside China, a few copies in Chinese are in private hands or kept in rare book libraries, such as at Harvard University or in Japan.

Apart from the general unavailability of the text, textual problems also abound. Helmut Martin has a detailed list of the various editions in his *Li Li-weng über Das Theater*.[2] The late Professor Kuhn in his German translation of the novel made a primary distinction between Edition A, a Japanese woodblock edition in four volumes, and Edition B, a movable type reprint of the so-called *Kuei-yu* edition, also in four volumes and amply illustrated, which was included in *Hsieh-ch'un-yüan ts'ung-kan*. Kuhn accepts the attribution of the authorship to Li Yü.[3]

Kuhn's belief that Li Yü was the author has, however, provoked counterarguments. If the novel was published in 1633, in his review of Kuhn's translation Professor Hightower argues that: "it makes the author of this pornographic masterpiece a twenty-two-year-old prodigy. One would hesitate to say such a thing is impossible, but it seems to me almost an axiom that while young men read pornography, it is not they who write it. In short, I do not see that Li Yü's authorship of *Jou P'u T'uan* is probable in terms of the available evidence. It is possible, of course, but under the circumstances it might have been better to leave his name off the title page."[4] Supporting Hightower, Professor Jeremey Ingalls opines that: "There is even some internal evidence, at least as apposite as Robert Graves' thesis about the author of the *Odyssey*, that the *hsien-sheng* who composed *Ju P'u T'uan* might have been a woman."[5]

Taking into consideration the judgments of some eminent Chinese and Western scholars and comparing the novel to Li Yü's other works, we are inclined to think that Li was very likely the author, even though the question will continue to be a matter of debate among scholars. Our basic reasons are: (1) In the preface to his *Miscellaneous Records of the Tsai Garden (Tsai-yüan tsa-chih),* Liu T'ing-chi, a contemporary of Li Yü, made the following remarks about Li Yü's writings: "Li Li-weng was the outstanding dramatic poet of the age. His works are extremely diverse, including ten plays *(ch'uan-chi), A Temporary Lodge for My Leisure Thoughts, Drama Without Sound,* and *Prayer Mat of Flesh.* In all his writings he was most original in both concept and language."[6] There is no reason to think that Liu's remarks were made casually, even though he did not claim personal acquaintance with Li. (2) In *A Brief History of Chinese Fiction,* Lu Hsün, a well-known writer and a foremost critic of the history of Chinese fiction, wrote: *"The Human Cassock [Jou p'u-t'uan],* which judging by its style may be the work of Li Yü, is comparatively good."[7] (3) Sun K'ai-ti, an outstanding modern expert on the bibliographical history of Chinese fiction in general, and on the life and works of Li Yü in particular, said of the novel: "An anonymous Ch'ing novel. . . . This is rather the best of the pornographic novels. The record found in the *Tsai-yüan tsa-chih* attributing this work to Li Yü is probably not far off."[8] (4) Helmut Martin in *Li Li-weng über Das Theater* and in *Li Yü ch'üan-chi (Complete Works of Li Yü)*[9] and Van Gulik in *Sexual Life in Ancient China* both attribute the authorship to Li Yü.[10]

In sum, most critics agree that Li Yü was the author. Though Professor Hightower's doubts are interesting, we can hardly concur with his statement that Li might have been too young to write the book. Works by young geniuses, such as those by Li Ho (791–817), Keats and Byron, Stephen Crane, and others are commonplace in literature and in the other arts. A Chinese example is the Ming playwright, Lu Ts'ai (fl. 1530) who wrote his famous *The Bright*

Pearl (Ming-chu chi) at eighteen. As to Hightower's second point, there is little evidence about which age groups read pornography. Some sociological studies have shown that it is more likely that old men read pornography while young men produce it. Moreover, by no means was Li Yü an ordinary or conventional man. As a youth, his interest in women and erotica far exceeded his interest in formal learning, as evidenced by his frequent references to sex and sexual behavior in either his prose works, such as *A Temporary Lodge,* or in the short stories in *Drama Without Sound* and *Twelve Towers.*

More specifically, there are similarities in the conception of the characters in his short stories and in the *Prayer Mat of Flesh.* For instance, among his lovers, Ch'u Ch'i-lang in "Tower of Rolling Clouds" shares many characteristics with the Before Midnight Scholar *(Wei-yang Sheng),* the protagonist in *Prayer Mat.* For example, the former falls on his knees begging Neng Hung, a maid-servant, to accept his love, while the latter kneels outside the Bowstringer God Temple to attract the attention of three departing ladies (Chapter 5). Again, Ch'ü, the lover in "Tower of Summer Comfort" uses an imported "thousand-mile mirror" (a telescope) to spy on women living within its range, and the Before Midnight Scholar rents a guest room at the Bowstringer God Temple to spy on the women devotees visiting the temple (Chapter 5).

Finally, among the puritanical fathers, Mr. Kuan in "Tower of Joining Reflections" acts like a twin brother to Dr. Iron Door *(T'ieh-fei tao-jen)* in *Prayer Mat.* Mr. Kuan is described as a man of very high moral standards. To avoid contact with his frivolous brother-in-law who lives next door, he erects a stone wall projecting high above the pond in his backyard; and to protect his daughter from arousing the interest of his nephew (her cousin), he insists that no close relatives be allowed within the inner quarters. Likewise, Dr. Iron Door is an equally strict man in his training of his daughter, who at age sixteen has hardly ever set foot outside the family compound, and never ventures out, not even to the temples. It appears that both Kuan and Dr. Iron Door subscribe to the principle of the separation of the sexes which had begun to be practiced in earnest in the Ming period.[11] Kuan's extreme measures only encourage others to plot against him and to make him a victim of their schemes. Similarly, Dr. Iron Door's inflexible and uncompromising moral stance first exposes his daughter to the interest of a rake and then to an avenger who is only interested in destroying Dr. Iron Door's family name. In both instances, Li stresses the futility of preventing the sexes from mingling.

There are also similarities in plot construction. First, the incident of invoking the divine in "Tower of Ten Nuptial Winecups" and the presence of an instructor of sex techniques in "An Official, Patronizing a Prostitute, Hears the Complaint of Her Former Customer" also appear in *Prayer Mat*.[12] Second, the author's penchant for numbers, such as his naming the *seven* schemes of a woman in "A Female Ch'en P'ing . . . ," and the *three* policies of buying and *three* other policies of nonselling adopted by the *three* shopkeepers in "Tower of Collected Elegance" is repeated in Monk Lonely Summit's (*Ku-feng chang-lao*) *three* self-imposed restrictions, and in the *five* principles of nonstealing adopted by K'un-lun's Rival (*Sai K'un-lun*), a noble thief.[13] Third, Scholar Chiang in "A Handsome Man, Trying to Avoid Sex Scandals, Manages to Create Them" lives next door to a young woman. The two houses adjoin each other and only a thin partition separates their bedrooms, a fact which provokes the young woman's father-in-law to file false charges of adultery against her and Scholar Chiang. In *Prayer Mat* the Before Midnight Scholar lives next door to a young woman, Scent Cloud (*Hsiang Yün*), one of the six women in the novel. In fact, only a similar thin partition divides his study from her boudoir. This proximity soon leads to their mutual involvement.[14] Fourth, when Yü in "Tower of the Returning Crane" returns home after years of exile in the land of the Tartars, he fully expects an anxious wife to await him at the door, but there is no sight of her:

He knew that she was bashful and thought that she might be waiting for him in the room. After he paid his respects to his father-in-law, he was ready to enter his own bedroom. Then he saw a curtain hanging in the middle of the inner hall of the reception room and a little piece of paper attached to the curtain. Approaching closer, he read with terror: "This is the coffin of Mrs. Pearl Yü." Breaking out in a cold sweat, he pulled his father-in-law to one side and demanded to know what was going on. Tearfully, Mr. Kuan said: "Ever since you left, Pearl counted the days until your return. She washed her face everyday with tears. After a few days she became ill. All the doctors diagnosed her case as melancholia caused by worries and anxieties, and it could only be cured by the return of her kin. . . . Utterly distraught, she refused to eat anything and starved to death. That was three years ago. She left instructions that she not be buried until you returned. . . ."[15]

Similarly, when the Before Midnight Scholar returns home from his adventures elsewhere, he meets his father-in-law instead of his wife.

The Before Midnight Scholar entered the inner hall or reception hall, greeted his father-in-law, sat down and asked how his father-in-law and his wife had been. Dr. Iron Door sighed and said: "I am quite well, but my daughter became ill soon after you left home. She could neither eat nor sleep, developed a serious case of melancholia, and died within that year." As he uttered the last sentence, Dr. Iron Door broke down and wept. The Before Midnight Scholar wondered aloud: "Could such a strange thing have happened?" Then he too beat his breast and wept. After a wave of weeping, he asked his father-in-law: "Where is the coffin? Has she been buried?" "No, the casket is still in the spare room. I was waiting for you before I made a final decision." Then the Before Midnight Scholar asked that he be taken to the spare room. Once inside it he prostrated himself on top of the casket and resumed his weeping.[16]

Again, the circumstances in both cases are nearly identical: the cause of death is melancholia and both women remain unburied. In addition, some of the wording is also identical. In "Tower of the Returning Crane," Li Yü uses *chung t'ing* ("reception room") and *yu yü* ("melancholia"); in *Prayer Mat*, we also find *chung t'ang* ("reception room") and *yu yü* ("melancholia").

There are similarities in the usage of expressions. For instance:

1) Reference to the same name. "Hui tao-jen," a sobriquet of the Taoist Immortal Lü, is found in both "Tower of Self-reformation" and in *Prayer Mat*.[17]

2) Identical similes. The phrase, "with a waist like Shen Yüeh's," is mentioned in "Tower of Collected Elegance" and in *Prayer Mat*.[18]

3) Similar allusions. References to "Ch'en P'ing" in *Drama Without Sound* and in *Prayer Mat*.[19]

4) Identical expressions. In "Tower of Rolling Clouds" and in *Prayer Mat* we find the lines: "What men plot together in secret/ Heaven hears like thunder."[20]

5) Uncommon and nearly identical expressions. In "Tower of Rolling Clouds" we read the following: "Chung-yüan yu liao, pang-yen yeh yu liao, chih k'o hsi mei yu t'an-hua." ("There is a number one and there is also a number two successful candidate in the imperial examination, but unfortunately, there is no number three").[21] In *Prayer Mat* we find: "Ch'i yu yu liao pang-yen t'an-hua, erh wu chuang-yüan chih li?" ("Is it possible that there are numbers two

and three in the imperial examination and no number one?")[22] Even more strikingly similar expressions are the following: In "A Male Mother Meng Changes His Residence Three Times to Protect His Foster Child": "Shui-lang hsiao-chieh t'a-yeh hsiao-chieh, Shui-lang ta-pien t'a-yeh ta-pien" ("Whenever Shui-lang did a small convenience [to urinate], he also did a small convenience; whenever Shui-lang did a big convenience [to evacuate the bowels], he too did a big convenience").[23] In *Prayer Mat* we read: "P'eng-yu hsiao-chieh t'a-yeh shui-ch'ü hsiao-chieh, ta-pien t'a-yeh ken-ch'ü ta-pien" ("Whenever a friend did a small convenience he also followed to do a small convenience, a big convenience he also followed with a big convenience").[24]

Reflecting his apparent interest in the theater, Li Yü uses theatrical terms and expressions generously in both *Twelve Towers* and *Prayer Mat*. Helmut Martin has particularly noted references to *hsi-wen* ("words of a play"), *cheng-sheng* ("protagonist"), *mo-chiao* ("supporting actor"), and pointed out that there are other examples too numerous to be listed in detail.[25]

It seems to us that all this reasonably establishes the authorship of *Prayer Mat of Flesh*. Now we shall proceed to examine (1) its relationship to the Chinese pornographic genre and, (2) more importantly, its artistic achievement.

II   Prayer Mat of Flesh *and the Pornographic Genre*

Though the popular conceptions of the Chinese as a very modest and prudish people is widespread, Van Gulik points out that the Chinese:

did indeed since early times give a great deal of attention to sex matters. Their observations are embodied in the "handbooks of sex," manuals teaching the householder how to conduct his relations with his womenfolk. These books existed already two thousand years ago, and were widely studied till about the 13th century. Thereafter Confucianist puritanism gradually restricted the circulation of literature of this genre. And after the advent of the Ch'ing dynasty in 1644 A.D. this puritanism, strengthened by political and emotional factors, resulted in the above-mentioned secretiveness about sex matters that obsessed the Chinese ever afterwards. . . .[26]

In support of his arguments, Van Gulik cites at random the existence of many such handbooks: *True Classic of the Complete Union (Chi-chi chen-ching), Record of the Bedchamber (Fang-nei chi),*

Discourses on the Cultivation of the True Essence (Hsiu-chen yen-yi), Admirable Discourses of the Plain Girl (Su-nü miao-lun), and *Ars Amatoria of Master Tung-hsüan (Tung-hsüan tzu),* an ancient handbook of sex. In addition, there were, *Poetical Essays on the Supreme Joy (Ta-lo fu),* the *Ocean of Iniquities of Monks and Nuns (Seng-ni nieh-hai),* and *The Fairies' Cavern (Yu-hsien k'u),* a short story already discussed in Chapter 2.[27] Moreover, the immediate precursors of *Prayer Mat of Flesh* were *Biography of Master Ju-yi (Ju-yi-chüan chuan), Unofficial History of the Embroidered Couch (Hsiu-t'a yeh-shih),* and *Biography of a Foolish Woman (Ch'ih-p'o-tzu chuan).* These three titles were all published before the *Prayer Mat of Flesh* and references are made to them in Chapter 3 of the *Prayer Mat.*

The existence of these handbooks, erotic texts, and pornographic novels does not indicate that they were readily available to the general public. A popular legend has it that *The Golden Lotus (Chin P'ing Mei)* was written by Wang Shih-chen (1526–1590), a great literary talent and historian, "to avenge the death of his father for which the evil minister Yen Shih-fan was mainly responsible. Because Yen was addicted to pornography, Wang poisoned the lower corner of every page of his completed manuscript and submitted it to him. As Yen mechanically moistened his fingertip with his own saliva to turn the pages, he eventually swallowed enough poison to cause his death."[28] The truth of the legend is not nearly as important as its indication of the rareness of pornographic materials and their unavailability even to government ministers.

III   Prayer Mat of Flesh: *Structure*

The handbooks dealt primarily with "the cosmic significance of the sexual union," with preliminary sex play, the sexual act, the therapeutic aspects thereof, the selection of partners for sexual satisfaction, and with various recipes and prescriptions.[29] But they were often repetitive and their writing dull and lifeless. On the other hand, *Prayer Mat of Flesh* not only offers the standard fare of a Chinese pornographic book, but it also offers the psychological insights and the other belletristic achievements usually found in literary masterpieces.

Compared to *The Golden Lotus,* its more famous sister, *Prayer Mat* has apparent similarities and differences. Thematically, Professor Kuhn points out, both books deal with erotic excesses, and superficially, the "heroes" in both books each have six partners. However, Kuhn perceptively notes that *Prayer Mat* is a better work in its treatment "of the hidden corners of erotic experience," in its portrayal of character and handling of psychological details, and in its brief and precise descriptions of external features such as those related to architecture and dress.[30] Professor C. T. Hsia, in comparing the two books, notes that *Prayer Mat* is "a work of greater novelistic competence and purity." Unlike *The Golden Lotus* with its generous inclusion of songs, poems, and other digressions related to the storyteller's conventions, Hsia points out that *Prayer Mat* uses a lively narrative style, and each chapter contains well-conceived scenes, realistic dialogue, and comic action—the combination carrying the story to a logical and dramatic ending.[31]

Structurally, Chapter 1 is a "preamble of didactic coherence."[32] It is one of the few existing essays in Chinese literature on sex. Clearly recognizing the importance of sex and its role in affecting a person's mental and physical well-being, the author wittily compares sexual pleasures with the consumption of ginseng roots. Extending his metaphor, he favors "homegrown" to "foreign" articles, the former being a person's wife or concubine—who proffer convenience, clean conscience, and unalloyed happiness—and the latter, professional prostitutes or illicit lovers. Intimacy with these latter, he feels, returns nothing but the loss of time and money, and feeling of remorse.

The remaining nineteen chapters can be divided into three parts. Part I begins with Chapter 2. In Chapter 2 the Before Midnight Scholar *(Wei-yang Sheng)*, the main character, brags to Monk Lonely Summit *(Ku-feng Chang-lao)* of his scholarly attainments and his desire to have the most beautiful women as his lovemates. The monk warns him of the punishments and retributions generally awaiting seducers of women. Unconvinced, the young hero leaves the monk and begins his pursuit of sexual adventures. In Chapter 3 the hero marries Noble Scent *(Yü-hsiang)*, the only daughter of Dr. Iron Door, a man noted for his aloofness in temperament and character as well as for his moral rectitude. The hero successfully overcomes Noble Scent's sexual inhibitions by introducing her to erotic literature. Chapter 4 finds the hero leaving Noble Scent to search for greater sexual conquests. He meets and becomes a sworn brother to the unusual thief, K'un-lun's Rival *(Sai K'un-lun)*. In Chapter 5 the hero rents a guest room in a temple where he spies on female devotees who come to worship the Bowstringer God. He keeps a journal of all the desirable women and of their characteristics. By Chapter 6 the hero, in exchanging information with K'un-lun's Rival, discovers the inadequacy of his sexual organ. We find him humiliated in Chapter 7; he secures the help of an itinerant physician who performs an operation, the purpose of which is to make him a much more powerful "instrument." Finally, in Chapter 8, following four months of strict abstinence from sex, the hero is now ready to benefit from the operation. His altered "equipment" is matchless in its potency.

In Part II, Chapter 9, we are introduced to Aroma (*Yen-fang*), the wife of Honest Ch'üan (*Ch'üan Lao-shih*), a silk merchant; here she is seduced by the hero, with the assistance of K'un-lun's Rival. In Chapter 10 the hero first "devastates" a neighbor lady of Aroma's before engaging Aroma in a fierce battle of lovemaking. Aroma is convinced she has made a wise decision in sacrificing her honor for a most worthwhile paramour. Complications arise in Chapter 11. Honest Ch'üan, the silk merchant, returns from his business trip. Suspicious of his wife, he learns incorrectly from neighbors that K'un-lun's Rival has been cuckolding him. Realizing that he has neither the money nor the power to resist the thief, he proposes to sell Aroma to K'un-lun's Rival, who buys her and presents her to the hero. In Chapter 12 Aroma becomes pregnant. Thus ends the first phase of Part II. The hero discovers that Scent Cloud, a woman whom he had seen earlier at the Bowstringer God temple, is actually his next-door neighbor. Affair with Scent Cloud begins. A secondary plot unfolds in Chapter 13. Honest Ch'üan finds out that he has been cuckolded by the Before Midnight Scholar and not by K'un-lun's Rival. He thirsts for revenge. Selling his belongings, he journeys to the home town of his enemy, becomes a servant to Dr. Iron Door, and marries one of the latter's maidservants. In Chapter 14 Honest Ch'üan seduces Noble Scent, the abandoned wife of the Before Midnight Scholar, and gets her pregnant. Meanwhile, in Chapter 15 Scent Cloud apprises the hero of three other pretty women, and introduces him to two of them: Lucky Pearl (*Jui-chu*) and Lucky Jade (*Jui-yü*). Most unselfishly, she allows her friends to share the sexual wonders the hero can provide. In Chapter 16, while visiting Lucky Pearl and Lucky Jade, Auntie Ch'en (*Hua-ch'en* or *Ch'en-ku*), the third woman, discovers the hero naked, hiding in a trunk. She has him transported to her house and monopolizes him for a whole week before returning him to the others. Finally, in Chapter 17, Auntie Ch'en devises love games for all to play. Unfortunately, she gets trapped in the game. Thus ends Part II.

In Part III, Chapter 18, the complete degradation of Noble Scent begins. Having eloped with Honest Ch'üan from her father's house because of her pregnancy, she has a miscarriage on the road. She is sold by Honest Ch'üan to a brothel in Peking and soon becomes one of the most sought-after prostitutes in town. Her fame spreads far and wide, drawing the husbands of Scent Cloud, Lucky Pearl, and Lucky Jade to her chamber while the men are in the capital on business. In Chapter 19 the Before Midnight Scholar bids goodbye to his five women and goes home. His father-in-law tells him that his wife died of melancholia some time ago. After mourning his wife, he leaves for Peking with the intention of patronizing the famous prostitute whom everyone has been talking about. When the prostitute recognizes him, she takes her own life, out of shame and regret. The hero discovers to his horror that the dead prostitute was Noble Scent, his wife. In Chapter 20, fully recognizing the evil he has done to himself and to others, the hero joins Monk Lonely Summit and becomes a disciple of Buddha. Still unable to assuage his sexual drives, he castrates himself. Soon Honest Ch'üan and K'un-lun's Rival come to the same realization and become followers of Buddha and disciples of Monk Lonely Summit.

In these twenty chapters the author never loses sight of the unity of the novel. There are few digressions. Every scene is constructed in such a way to advance the central action of the story. Unity is achieved through (1) a successful combination of two plots; (2) the use of character analogies; and (3) the use of recurring metaphors.

IV *Combination of the Two Plots*

The novel has two separate plots: the sexual adventures of the hero and of Honest Ch'üan. Though the two plots could be independent of each other, they are connected through the roles assigned to Monk Lonely Summit and Noble Scent. The role of Monk Lonely Summit is largely structural. Appearing in the first and the last chapters, he serves as a moral arbitrator in an amoral world of sin, violence, and sex orgies. In the end, he accepts the Before Midnight Scholar, Honest Ch'üan, and K'un-lun's Rival as his disciples. On the other hand, Noble Scent has a much more complex role. She has a central position in the novel. As the daughter of Dr.

Iron Door, the wife of the Before Midnight Scholar, the mistress of
Honest Ch'üan, and lastly the common whore who serves the husbands of Scent Cloud, Lucky Jade, and Lucky Pearl, she is linked to
all the male characters except K'un-lun's Rival. While living, she is
exploited by her father, her husband, her paramour, and to a lesser
degree by all her patrons. And she is made to pay for the evils
committed against her by her male companions. In death she becomes the unwitting agent of her husband's and her paramour's
moral salvation. Ironically, it is her utter degradation as she changes
from a demure maiden to a notorious prostitute that saves those who
have worst exploited her.

V *Character Analogies*

In addition to the roles assigned to Monk Lonely Summit and to
Noble Scent, the two plots are held together by the use of character
analogies. Though of different social and cultural backgrounds, the
Before Midnight Scholar and Honest Ch'üan have much in common. Both have extremely efficient sexual instruments which en-
able them to win the affections of their women. The former's is the
result of a surgical operation; the latter's a gift of birth. Both have
sexual relationships with and impregnate the other's wife, though
the resulting offspring die. Moreover, on behalf of the Before Midnight Scholar, K'un-lun's Rival purchases Honest Ch'üan's wife with
money, and later Honest Ch'üan sells the Before Midnight Scholar's
wife to a brothel, also for money. In the end, the three men repent
and become the disciples of Monk Lonely Summit.

The women in the novel are also in similar situations. Noble Scent
is seduced by Honest Ch'üan while her husband is away from home;
Aroma by the Before Midnight Scholar when her husband is away
on business; Scent Cloud, Lucky Jade, and Lucky Pearl, as well as
Auntie Ch'en, all become easy targets for the Before Midnight
Scholar because their husbands are either away from home or dead.

VI *Recurring Metaphors*

Two types of recurring metaphors abound in the novel. The author's apparent interest in the theater is reflected in theatrical references. The Before Midnight Scholar has been compared to the protagonist in a play and Monk Lonely Summit to a supporting actor by
an anonymous critic whose comments are found at the end of each
chapter. The presence of these comparisons underlies the author's

belief that the world is much like a stage and that characters in fiction are like actors performing roles on the stage.

Another metaphor used to describe the hero's sexual experiences is to compare them with the trials of a schoolboy under a tutor or of a scholar at an examination. One example is:

If you apply a vernal ointment to a naturally powerful instrument, it is exactly as though a gifted and well-prepared second-degree holder [*chü-jen*] should take a ginseng stimulant just before his examination. He will feel doubly fresh and alert, and his dissertation will pour out of its own accord. On the other hand, a lover whose implement is feeble by nature will no more be fortified by ointments than an ignorant and untalented first-degree holder [*hsiu-ts'ai*] would be helped by drugs—even if he consumed whole pounds of them before his examination.[33]

Apart from the uses of a successful combination of two plots, character analogies, and recurring metaphors, the novel is also noted for its witty comments, comic dialogue, well-conceived humorous or key scenes, the use of irony in place descriptions and character portrayal, the creation of one character, the hero, and the exploration of sexuality as a theme.

VII *Witty Comments and Comic Dialogue*

The author's comments often display a sharp and clever wit. Note his rationale for the desirability of nearsightedness in women:

If a lewd woman has sharp eyes and is able to see all the handsome men, it is likely that her heart would be moved and she would be constantly tempted. Therefore the Creator has made her eyes nearsighted, allowing her to see no one but her husband. Even if a paragon of masculine handsomeness such as a likeness of P'an An or Sung Yü approaches her, she won't notice his presence, and therefore, be spared from conjugal misconduct. From time immemorial, the great majority of nearsighted women is free from scandal, specifically because of their nearsightedness.[34]

In another passage, the author talks about two different types of women:

For a woman to be beautiful to look upon, she must possess three qualities: she must be thin rather than plump, tiny rather than large, frail and modest rather than robust and forward. Women in paintings all have waists like thin willow branches, bodies so thin that they disappear within their clothes, and none of the models is ever plump or stout. . . . But for a woman to be enjoyable, she must be plump rather than thin, large rather than tiny, robust and forward rather than frail or modest. Why must she possess these qualities? In cohabitation, when a man lies on top of a woman, first, he looks for softness; second, he looks for compatibility of body sizes; and third, he looks for a partner able to withstand his weight. Lying on top of a skinny woman is like lying on top of a stone slate, and his whole body will feel sore. . . .[35]

And he provides a philosophy of theft, expounded by K'un-lun's Rival: "I spare people in times of family death or festivities; my friends; those who have already been robbed; and unsuspecting souls who take no precautions against theft."[36]

Unexpected, also, is Scent Cloud's comparison of the Before Midnight Scholar's equipment to bean curd: "Nothing is so hard and solid [as bean curd], neither gold nor silver nor copper nor iron. Metals may seem ever so hard, but in fire they soften and melt. The only thing that resists fire and does not melt is bean curd. The greater the heat, the harder it becomes. That's just how it is with his utensil, and I have therefore compared it to bean curd."[37]

Witty dialogue in the novel ranges from the Before Midnight Scholar bragging to the Monk Lonely Summit: "I have no wish to boast, but I feel justified in saying that my learning, my memory, my gift of comprehension, and my literary style are of the first order. The literary lights of our day are all mediocrities. . . . I wish to become a true literary giant. I intend to read all the rare books, meet all the geniuses, and visit all the scenic spots. Then I will seclude myself and write a book and go down in the literary history of my country as the first master of prose writing . . .";[38] to the moral indignation of modest Noble Scent when shown a porno-graphic book: "Where did you get such an inauspicious item? If you leave it here, it sullies and befouls the atmosphere of my chaste chamber. Quickly tell the maidservant to burn it";[39] or the implied comparison of women to different grades of meat. Witness the fol-lowing exchange between K'un-lun's Rival and the Before Midnight Scholar:

"Let me ask you a question? Do you prefer them buxom or slender?" asked K'un-lun's Rival. "It all depends. Buxom or slender, both can have charm. But by buxom I do not mean so fat that her dress bursts at the seams; nor by slender do I mean so skinny that her bones pierce holes in her gown. It is all a matter of degree," replied the Before Midnight Scholar. Then K'un-lun's Rival said: "Fine. In that case all three would meet your wishes. Let me ask you one more question: Do you prefer them passionate or prudish?"[40]

VIII   *Well-conceived Humorous Scenes*

Li Yü's humorous scenes are of two different types. The first, short and amusing, provides glimpses of a character and evokes in the reader surprise and/or pleasure; the second, more elaborate, demonstrates the author's ability to create scenes of sustained hilarity.

Of the human sensory organs, none can be compared in usefulness to the eyes. Much of the fun in the novel is provided by what one sees or does not see. In Chapter 9, after having engaged Aroma's neighbor woman in a protracted sexual battle in total darkness, the Before Midnight Scholar suddenly "turned his head and looked carefully at his partner. She was a most ugly 'monster.' A face riddled with pockmarks, head full of dull pasty hair, the color of her skin resembling unwashed *Chin-hua* ham. He screamed in horror."[41] In direct contrast is Auntie Ch'en's feelings of surprise as she sees "a smooth-looking and snow-white naked man sleeping inside a trunk. Across his thigh was a 'flesh stick.' Its size was so impressive even when it was soft that she had no idea of what it would be like when it hardened."[42]

A scene of extreme delight is provided the Before Midnight Scholar as he spies beautiful Scent Cloud bending to pick up the lid of the "horse bucket" from the floor: "She exposed her well-rounded moon hills and her hidden vale of pleasure."[43] In Chapter 14 Honest Ch'üan gets an equally delightful view. Knowing that Honest Ch'üan is outside the window peeping in, Noble Scent deliberately makes herself as provocative as possible when she takes a bath: "She turned to face the window, fully revealing her two 'flesh peaks' and her vale, allowing him a chance to feast his eyes. Worried that he might not be able to see her vale submerged in water, she raised herself in the tub and spread her legs. . . ."[44]

Apart from the above-mentioned brief scenes providing the reader with transitory moments of disgust or ecstasy, there are extended scenes of humor, even of hilarity. For instance, there is seduction in Chapter 8. It begins with an unsuspecting Aroma, who as the wife of Honest Ch'üan is happy and contented with her domestic life. When K'un-lun's Rival and the Before Midnight Scholar visit her shop ostensibly to buy silk, she maintains a strict composure and gives them no encouragement. However, her severity and self-control falter as she hears compliments paid to her by the Before Midnight Scholar in his pleasant voice. Her resistance is put to a further strain when she notices his fine hand, and it collapses completely when she sees his handsome face. Her severity thaws into a friendly smile, inviting further attentions from her seducer-to-be. All at once, she becomes ready and willing. Later, when he touches and gently presses her hand, she reciprocates by slightly scratching the back of his. When he pays her a silver nugget for the silk and comments that it is "sterling silver," an allusion to his own person, she replies with equally vague but seductive cleverness: "It is all silver all right. I'm afraid it is good to look at but not useful."[45]

Remarkable for its witty exchanges between seducer and seduced is the seduction scene detailing how the attentions of a truly worthy lover gradually weaken Aroma's self-restraint; whereas the love contest devised by Auntie Ch'en in Chapter 17 is a scene of fun and hilarity. Considering herself the queen of Erosdom, Auntie Ch'en suggests to her young friends that a contest be organized using cards. The deck of cards is placed face down and each of the participants must pick the topmost card and then act out the position represented on its face—with, of course, the help of the Before Midnight Scholar. Once a player has picked a card, she is forbidden to exchange it. Her regulations regarding the duration of the combat are equally autocratic and strict. The participant who imitates the picture most authentically and elegantly is to be declared winner. When Lucky Pearl asks what if she should deviate from the model, Auntie declares that she will be condemned to three punitive cups of wine and must begin again from the beginning. Without much reflection, she adds that if one should commit any breach of the regulations or try to cheat in any way, the others may set up a loud cry of protest.

But when Auntie chooses the objectionable "I want to get married" position, through the clever schemes of her young friends, she pleads fervently for mercy:

"Dear friends, please," she begged, "consider if this can be done. Can his 'thing' do such a thing? Please think again." All the women replied,

"No. . . . Let you off? What if one of us had picked this same card? Would you let her off? You said yourself that the cards could not be changed, and that you knew all the cards. . . . Off with your clothes. Or shall we undress you by force?" Then they turned to the Before Midnight Scholar: "Hey, you. What are you deputy for? Why didn't you open your mouth or do something? . . ."[46]

As the Before Midnight Scholar pleads for Auntie Ch'en, he only arouses the ire of the young women who reply: "Nonsense [*Fang P'i*]! If she is allowed to get away with punitive cups, we should have been allowed to drink them instead of performing the acts. Do you suppose we enjoyed the show we put on?"[47] After much argument, Auntie Ch'en allows her clothes to be removed. Then reluctantly, but spurred on by encouraging remarks from all sides, she takes the position on the edge of a divan: "face and belly down, near portal upraised."[48] The ultimate result of the love contest she herself has devised turns out to be a most traumatic experience for her. She has to spend three days in bed, racked with fever and tortured by a painful red swelling on her posterior.

IX *Key Scenes*

Apart from the well-conceived humorous scenes, there are others important to the dramatic intensity of the novel. The initial debate between Monk Lonely Summit and the Before Midnight Scholar in Chapter 2 draws a sharp contrast between the views of an old sophisticated monk who has seen through the "red dust" of the world and those of a young inexperienced lad ready to face the world. The scene ends with the monk's warning to the young man in a *gatha:*

> Cast away the leather sack,
> Sit on the prayer mat of flesh.
> Repent in time,
> Lest the coffin closes over you.[49]

The *gatha* serves as the moral criteria by which the hero's subsequent actions are to be judged.

Pivotal to transforming a self-confident braggart into a pathetic juvenile is the scene in Chapter 7. To make sure that K'un-lun's Rival has told him the truth about the different sizes of human "equipment," the Before Midnight Scholar becomes very prying.

He follows his fellow students to the restrooms to compare their sizes with his. On the basis of extensive comparison, he realizes that his friend has not exaggerated. Neither among acquaintances nor strangers is he able to find an "instrument" as unimpressive as his.

The scene with the great dramatic tension occurs in Chapter 19, and it signals the denouement of the novel. It begins with the hero's visit to the brothel in Peking and his asking for the service of its most famous prostitute, of whom he has heard a great deal. When she (Noble Scent) sees him from behind a screened window, she declines to serve him. But her madam insists that she do so. In desperation, she hangs herself in her boudoir with a silk sash from her waist. Growing impatient with his long wait, the hero kicks open the door and enters the boudoir, only to find a woman hanging there. He turns away in horror, without looking at the woman. His only thought is to be gone as quickly as possible, but his way is barred by the madam of the house. With the help of several assistants, she ties him up and puts him on a mat, side by side with the corpse which has meanwhile been cut down. There he is to lie until the police should come for him. Left alone with the dead woman and seized by morbid curiosity, he looks at her more closely. He is horrified to recognize her as his wife, Noble Scent; he then understands why his father-in-law told him that Noble Scent had died a long time ago and had even shown him her coffin. With the death of his first wife, the hero begins a life of repentance by joining Monk Lonely Summit as his disciple.

X   Irony

Li Yü excels not only in producing well-conceived scenes, but also in using irony as a literary device to show the discrepancies between what appears to be and what actually is. There are many examples of this in the novel. To cite one, although Dr. Iron Door's house is steeped in moral tradition, it is the place where the hero artfully introduces the pleasures of sex to his virginal wife. Her rapid transformation from a virtuous maiden to a wanton woman is a sign of the fragility of an artificially imposed moral order. Later, Honest Ch'üan's seduction of a willing Noble Scent represents a severe cracking of that moral foundation. And lastly, to preserve the appearance of that moral tradition from complete collapse, Dr. Iron Door lies to his son-in-law about his daughter's death. As for Dr. Iron Door himself, all his Neo-Confucian training and self-righteousness did not help him form a correct judgment of either his son-in-law or Honest Ch'üan. In fact, his "iron door" did not prevent his son-in-law from corrupting his daughter, seducer Honest Ch'üan from getting into his household, nor his daughter from eloping. There are other examples of irony. For instance, the temple where the Before Midnight Scholar stays is to him not a place of worship but one where he can spy on female devotees; and his guest room at the temple is not a place of study but one where homosexual orgies take place. Lastly, the brothel in Peking where only money and sex are important becomes the place of moral truth and reformation.

The author applies the use of irony to people as well. In the case of Honest Ch'üan, the irony is complete. His name is wrought with it, almost as ironical as the epithet given to "Honest Iago" by Othello. Honest Ch'üan, or Ch'üan Lao-shih, is known to everyone as a quiet and accommodating man who would not hurt a fly; he is also described as a candid soul, "incapable of imputing evil designs to his fellowmen, least of all to his esteemed regular customer. He was indeed fully deserving of his nickname Lao-shih, 'the guileless.' "[50] But in fact, it is only that his real self is well hidden. Discovering that he has been cuckolded by the Before Midnight Scholar, he swears vengeance. In a series of well-thought-out and executed plans, he sells his house and property and journeys to the hometown of his foe. Once there, he learns all he can about his enemy's father-in-law's household. Learning of Dr. Iron Door's miserliness, he figures this is something he can exploit. To gain admittance into the otherwise inaccessible household, he offers to rent Dr. Iron Door's land under terms most unfavorable to himself. Once employed by Dr. Iron Door, he works hard at farming, performs the housework, and otherwise impresses Dr. Iron Door with his solid qualities. Whenever he passes Noble Scent, the real object of his pursuit, he pretends to be unaware of her presence. In a few months' time, he has won Dr. Iron Door's complete confidence and is rewarded with one of the maidservants. Firmly entrenched in the family, he relinquishes his ascetic mask and openly professes an interest in Noble Scent. Whenever he passes her, he now gives her an appealing little glance. Having seduced and impregnated her, he elopes with her and his servant-wife. And as soon as Noble Scent miscarries his baby on the road, he mercilessly sells her and his servant-wife to a brothel in Peking. All his actions have been carried out with military precision. The "Lao-shih" that everyone has known is really a master of disguise, of relentless revenge, and of suppressed hatred. Chosen to manipulate the fate of others, he commits the same unforgivable sin which Roger Chillingworth committed in Hawthorne's *The Scarlet Letter* (1850): the willful abandonment of human kindness for the heartless pursuit of revenge.

XI *The Hero*

Besides the use of irony as a literary device, much of the strength of the book as Chinese literature derives from the creation of a successful rake. The Before Midnight Scholar meets the requirements Aristotle laid down in his description of the hero in the *Poetics*, among which are the qualities of an ordinary mortal. The Before Midnight Scholar exhibits human qualities, for instance, in boasting of his desire to be the number one scholar in the land and to marry the foremost beauty, and in regressing to a pathetic juvenile upon learning of the inadequacy of his sexual instrument. Witness his bitter laments to Heaven: "You are to be blamed for it all, Oh Prince of Heaven. If in your magnanimity you wished to favor me over other men, you should have favored me thoroughly. Why did you curse me with such a defect? Intelligence and good looks may be impressive but they are useless in combat."[51]

Further, we must consider how he resorts to human guile to find his bedmates: he rents a guest room at the Bowstringer God Temple and spies on the women devotees who come to worship. He keeps careful watch on the entrance to the temple and as soon as he sees women approaching, he hides behind the broad back of the deity's statue. Unseen, he is able to look through a gap that the sculptor left between the deity's sleeve and his gown. Inspecting the women devotees closely, he keeps a journal of each one's attire, figure, and other pertinent details.

Again, when occasion demands, he is capable of clownish behavior. Once when some pretty women are leaving the temple grounds, he kneels down and kowtows time after time, tapping his forehead on the ground just to draw their attention. In his dealings with women, he fabricates lies to fit every occasion. He explains to his innocent wife, for instance, that his purpose in introducing pornographic material to her is to prepare her for womanhood.

The Aristotelian hero must be "bigger than life," better and more virtuous than the average man. The Before Midnight Scholar is larger than life in his unmatched sexual prowess which makes him a giant among men; he is better and more virtuous than the average man in his ultimate potential for redemption. Once he realizes the evil he has done to others, he renounces the world to become a follower of Buddha and of Monk Lonely Summit. Unable to stifle his sexual desires, he manfully castrates himself. For him there is only a total commitment to absolutes; that is, a full "enjoyment" of what life offers or a complete rejection of that life.

In short, the Before Midnight Scholar's adventures follow the pattern of what R. W. B. Lewis defines as the Adamic experience: "the birth of the innocent, the foray into the unknown world, the collision with that world, 'the fortunate fall,' the wisdom and the maturity which suffering produced."[52] Moreover, he resembles Tom Jones, Candide, and even Byron's Don Juan in his ability to learn from experience. More sharply defined than Hsi-men Ch'ing in *The Golden Lotus,* he exhibits an exuberance that makes him the closest Chinese equivalent to the Byronic hero in his courtesy toward women, his strong sense of honor and guilt, and in his ability to elicit a sympathetic response from the reader.[53]

Prayer Mat of Flesh is a novel of many things. Besides being pornography, comedy, and satire, it is also a thoughtful exploration of the subject of sexuality, a topic largely neglected by Chinese writers. While pornography involves only a clinical description of the reproductive organs and the various ways of performing the sex act, sexuality examines their total impact on the complete human being. The author deals with sexuality as repressed in women and open in men.

XII *Sexuality as Theme*

The theme of repressed sexuality is represented primarily through Noble Scent, a "veritable epitome of maidenly virtue," born in a strict family and reared by a moralistic father. Due to her traditional upbringing, she wears "an armor of virginal modesty and reserve." Without any contact with the outside world or even with girlfriends, she has no interest in sex and sees it as sin or ugliness. At first she resists her husband's sexual advances with vigor. But once her sexuality is awakened she welcomes it. Following the departure of her husband, she feels deserted and takes refuge in reading a spicy book that her husband purchased for her in the early days of their marriage. But the book never satisfies any inner hunger, and she becomes an easy prey to Honest Ch'üan. He desires only to seduce her and then degrade her by one indignity after another; as the final indignity he sells her to a brothel in Peking.

Unlike her more famous counterpart, Golden Lotus, in the novel *The Golden Lotus*, Noble Scent is weak-willed and submissive and allows her father, her husband, and her paramour to exploit her totally. While Golden Lotus "sees nothing beyond sex,"[54] Noble Scent sees much beyond it. When she becomes pregnant with Honest Ch'üan's child, she sees her father's humiliation and the reputation of her family at stake and suggests elopement to Honest Ch'üan. After having been sold to a brothel, she adopts an alias. And when she sees her husband asking for her services, she takes her own life—a brave act of self-redemption. In death she finds solace and final triumph. She is the Persecuted Maiden, a projection of male guilt.

Noble Scent's tragic fate is the result of her family upbringing, her submissive nature, and her inability to cope with her aroused sexuality. Aroma has similar problems. The daughter of a private village scholar, she is first married to a college graduate who dies of neurasthenia and exhaustion after a year and a half of marriage. Married again, this time to Honest Ch'üan, she is at first happy with him, adopting an attitude of severity and condemning infidelity. For women to have affairs behind their husbands' backs is to her an offence against the ethical and social order. But her platitudes and moralistic talk are not enough of a barrier to protect her from the Before Midnight Scholar's seductive charm. Once involved with him and becoming aware of her hidden sexual desires, she resolves to win her freedom from her husband by making life utterly miserable for him. She scolds him for no reason; complains at every opportunity; makes him do all the housework during the day and multiplies her demands on him at night. In two months' time, she transforms a robust husband into an emaciated shadow of misery. But in destroying him she destroys herself. For in return she is rewarded with a lover who abandons her when she becomes pregnant; her fully aroused sexual desires, however, know no bounds and plunge her into further drastic acts. She elopes with a monk who holds up travelers and leaves her twin daughters behind; finally, she dies a cruel death at the hands of K'un-lun's Rival.

Besides Noble Scent and Aroma, Li Yü is equally sensitive to the pain of sexual deprivation in the other women. While their husbands cavort with prostitutes or other females of doubtful virtue, Scent Cloud, Lucky Jade, and Lucky Pearl might as well be abandoned and have to occupy their time with sexual fantasies. When the opportunity for an extramarital affair appears in the person of a robust young lover, they desert their conventional morality and indulge in an orgy of sexual pleasure. In the cases of Noble Scent and Aroma, their license leads to suicide and murder, and for the other women, indulgence leads to domestic chaos, marital dissatisfaction, and perhaps lifelong feelings of guilt and remorse.

Though men in traditional Chinese society had universal access to extramarital affairs, few of them had an understanding of what sex involves. The Before Midnight Scholar confuses it with the expression of his manhood and takes delight in the number of women he can have. Very much like his brother Hsi-men Ch'ing in *The Golden Lotus*, he becomes more interested in impressing women with his sexual prowess and in giving them pleasure than in receiving pleasure himself. Sex becomes a burden, a drudge, as he becomes a pleasure-machine serving and catering to the insatiable demands of his women. In the end it destroys him. Somewhat differently, Honest Ch'üan uses sex not so much as a source of pleasure to himself but as a potent weapon of revenge. It is his sexual prowess that endears him to Noble Scent, enabling him to revenge himself on the Before Midnight Scholar by seducing his wife. His attitude toward sex is just as misguided as the Before Midnight Scholar's, since he also fails to see it as a part of love. Equally removed from a healthy approach to sex is K'un-lun's Rival, whose noninvolvement with it makes him bloody and violent, as evidenced by his murder of Aroma.

In a world where love is nonexistent, lust is a raging fire that consumes everyone with a destructive power unimaginable to the characters themselves. However, with a saving stroke, the author offers the hope of salvation in the suicide of Noble Scent and the voluntary self-castration of the Before Midnight Scholar. Their self-sacrifices represent the human capacity for change and redemption in which Li Yü seems to have believed strongly. In the introductory remarks to the "Tower of Self-reformation" in *Twelve Towers* he states this belief unequivocally:

In the *Four Books* there is the following saying: "Even evil people, after controlling their thoughts, fasting and praying, may serve God." Controlling the thoughts, fasting and praying mean to *hui-t'ou* [to turn one's head]. How is it that evil people may yet serve God? To use a simile, to do good is like having fair weather; and to do evil is like having foul weather. On days when the weather is good, no one appreciates the sunshine; however, when it is raining, one longs to see the sun and would rejoice to see the weather change. . . . Good deeds of good people are seldom noticed. Doing good is more or less expected of them. . . . But for evil people to perform good deeds is most unusual. . . . Similarly, evil people, when reformed, are coveted by God.[55]

CHAPTER 6

Li's Dramatic Theory

I *Introduction*

DRAMA derives from dancing, and particularly from group folk dancing. Ancient Chinese records indicate that the earliest group dancing in that part of Asia originated with the Miao tribes in Yünnan and Kweichow provinces, from which developed dancing at temple sacrifices.[1] Although such "theatrical" activities as religious dances and court entertainments by clowns and acrobats are known to have existed in early China, drama is a late Chinese development. While the Roman empire watched and shouted at chariot races and gladiatorial contests, the Chinese admired wrestling, boxing, fencing, and tightrope walking. In the last years of the second century B.C., they watched song actors dressed as leopards, tigers, and other animals, and heard others performing solo roles or singing simple lyrics. All these activities can be considered the remote beginnings of drama in China.[2]

While Western drama originated in the Christian church, Chinese drama received its initial blessings from the rulers and the government. As singing and dancing assumed greater importance, the Hsüan-tsung emperor (r. 713–755), known as Ming-huang, of the T'ang dynasty established the famous Pear Garden and other centers for the training of actors. And the Sung rulers (960–1276) similarly supported actors. As these court amusements became public entertainment and gained greater popularity among the people, Sung dynasty theatrical performances were staged either in regular playhouses or on temporary stages set up for special occasions. The theatrical performances consisted of singing, dancing, instrumental music, and acrobatics, as well as a new theatrical show known as the variety play *(tsa-chü)*. Unfortunately, none of these plays is extant; in fact, nothing remains except a long list of titles, from which we

113

learn that the plays were historical, supernatural, literary or didactic, satirical, and farcical in nature. A typical Sung variety play had a prelude, a main play in one or two scenes, and a musical epilogue.[3]

Contemporaneous with the Sung variety play was the Southern drama *(Nan-hsi)*. It was, primarily, native to the people of the Southeast coast and gradually attained popularity in Wenchow and Hangchow. Consisting of a long sustained story in song and dialogue, it represented a significant improvement over other types of Sung theatrical compositions. The songs were arranged in sequence, written in simple and colloquial language, and vividly expressed, which realistically heightened the sentiments of the characters; dialogue was generally used to advance the action. In many cases the songs were noted for their naturalness and spontaneity of feeling, and the melodies were derived from popular tunes sung on street corners and in marketplaces. The verses were usually superior to the embellished and lifeless poems of the contemporary "literary" writers.[4]

Strangely, drama in China did not fully come of age until the non-Chinese Yüan dynasty (1234–1367) came to power. By abolishing the literary examination (which was not restored until 1314), the Mongol conquerors closed the traditional route for scholars to achieve fame and distinction and, as a substitute, forced them to take an interest in the writing of drama. However, an even more important reason, as suggested by Professor Stephen West, was that "drama, as a self-sustaining and self-developing tradition had, at this crucial point in time, simply matured to the point that it offered a suitable vehicle for literary expression."[5]

In terms of continuity, starting with the T'ang and Sung drama which had become more sophisticated with varied repertories and credible plots, the spectacular growth of Yüan drama could perhaps have been anticipated. But in form and structure, the Yüan plays were unique. Each had four distinct acts or song sequences, and might or might not include a "wedge" *(hsieh-tzu)* placed at the beginning or between two acts. The wedge was shorter and contained fewer songs than a regular act and was designed to solidify the structure of the play. Each act contained one song sequence of about ten lyrics of varying lengths; each lyric was limited to one repeated rhyming sound in the same tonality or key (in the musical scale), although different acts had different tonalities. All the lyrics were sung by the male and female lead characters, and singing was much more important than acting. The excellence of a play was judged by its poetry rather than by its plot or dialogue. Consequently, it contained little action. In most cases the dialogue was conventional and uninformative, and the humor crude and even accidental. Little is known about the playwrights of the Yüan period except that there were more than a hundred of them. We know very little about the lives of these playwrights, but the Yüan period bustled with theatrical activities. At least six to seven hundred plays were staged in a little over a century, but only a fourth of them are extant.[6]

A general decline of the drama occurred during the Ming dynasty. Drama became the specialty of leisured poets who were more interested in poetic flourishes than in the dramatic quality of their works; thus this kind of drama eventually lost the support of the people. These poets invented few new plots, but instead were content to rehash the old ones that came from historical sources or concerned semihistorical myths. However, two new types of drama soon appeared on the stage: (1) the *ch'uan-chi* play of forty or more scenes and (2) a much shorter play, containing sometimes only one scene. In addition, there emerged the K'un-shan drama, or *K'un-ch'ü*, which dominated the national stage by 1600, and the songs of which were sung to the tunes of the Soochow (Wu) dialect. Unlike the playwrights of an earlier period, most of the K'un-ch'ü writers were celebrities who wrote for fame rather than for profit.

T'ang Hsien-tsu (1550–1617), probably one of the most important Ming playwrights, stressed lyric sentiment and beauty to the neglect of the metrical requirements of the *ch'ü* songs. His rival, Shen Ching (1553–1610), emphasized the prosodic aspects of drama. There continued to exist, of course, professional men of the theater who were primarily interested in making a living. And, in the works of Li Yü, we see "the poetic talents of a literary writer, the musical skills of a virtuoso, and the professional knowledge of a man of the theater" all combined in one person.[7]

First, Li Yü was a playwright. He wrote at least ten plays, two of which, *Ordained by Heaven (Nai-ho t'ien)* and *Errors of the Kite (Feng-cheng wu)* are popular and delightful comedies, still loved by many. Second, he was a director and producer of plays. He organized his own family troupe of more than forty members and gave performances in different parts of China. Third, he was a critic whose dramatic theory encompassed his critiques of the works of his predecessors as well as his own concepts of playwriting, the production of plays, and the training of actors. In its scope and depth, it was unique in the history of Chinese drama criticism.

II *History of Drama Criticism*

To evaluate Li Yü's contributions to Chinese drama criticism properly, we must begin with a brief historical survey of drama criticism up to Li's time. Throughout the T'ang, Sung, Yüan, and Ming dynasties, there were indeed many books on dramatic poetry and songs, running commentaries or editors' notes, comments on scripts and theatrical performances, single critical prefaces, postcripts, letters and essays, and studies of different aspects of script writing and the composition of songs, biographical sketches of actors, as well as of the historical development of particular plays. However, most of these critical comments, especially those written during the T'ang and Sung dynasties, are disorganized, brief, and unsatisfactory.[8]

During the Yüan dynasty, there appeared Chou Te-ch'ing's *The Phonology of the Dialect of North China (Chung-yüan yin-yün*, compiled in 1324), a book on rhyme, sound discrimination, methods of using words, musical tones, and the ten rules to be followed in composing songs. Strictly speaking, *The Phonology* bears little relationship to drama criticism.[9] In addition, there were two other important books: Chung Ssu-ch'eng's *The Book of Ghosts (Lu-kuei pu)* and Yen-nan Chih-an's *The Book About Singing (Ch'ang lun)*. The first one stresses biographies of songwriters, and the second treats of ancient musicians and the major genres of classical drama.

During the Ming dynasty, there were Prince Chu Ch'üan's (1378–1448) *Handbook on the Orthodox Music of Supreme Harmony (T'ai-ho cheng-yin-p'u)*, which divides drama into twelve categories according to the themes; Tsang Mou-hsün's (fl. 1595) *Selections from the Yüan Drama (Yüan-ch'ü hsüan*, prefaced 1616); Hsü Wei's (1521–1593) *Notes on the Southern Drama (Nan-tz'u hsü-lu)*; Ho Liang-chün's (1506–1573) *Commentaries on Songs (Ch'ü-lun)*; Wang Shih-chen's (1528–1590) *The Rhetoric of Songs (Ch'ü-tsao)*; Lü T'ien-cheng's *Treatise on Drama (Ch'ü-pin*, prefaced 1610); Wang Chi-te's (d. 1623) *The Rules of Drama (Ch'u-lü)*; and Ling Meng-ch'u's (ca. 1584–1644) *Miscellaneous Notes on Drama (T'an-ch'ü tsa-cha)*. These critical studies emphasize music, the rhetoric of songs, and the literary merits of the language. These critics generally regarded drama as an extension of poetry and, with the possible exception of Wang Chi-te, they had little to say about acting.

During the early Ch'ing period there were Huang Chou-hsing's (1611–1680) *Side Talks on Drama Composition (Chih-ch'ü chih-yü)* and Liu T'ing-chi's (fl. 1676) *On Drama Studied at the Tsai Garden (Tsai-yüan ch'ü-chih)*. Huang addresses himself to the composition of *ch'ü* songs, and Liu records what he considers to be the essence of *ch'ü* songs and plays. However, only in Li Yü do we find China's first drama critic of note.[10]

III *Li's Dramatic Theory*

Li's dramatic theory as stated in *A Temporary Lodge for My Leisure Thoughts* is divided into three major parts: the play itself *(tzu-ch'ü)*, problems of staging *(yen-hsi)*, and bad theatrical practices *(t'uo-t'ao)*. As for the play itself, he speaks of plot construction, the use of language, music and prosody, dialogue, comic elements, and dramatic construction. Regarding the problems of staging, he mentions the selection of scripts, adapting or abridging long plays into short scenes, the training of singers, and the teaching of elocution. And lastly, concerning bad theatrical practices, he points out unacceptable practices in actors' costumes, voice training, language, and comic jests.[11]

A cursory examination of Li's dramatic theory reveals little about his contributions to the Chinese theater or to the development of drama criticism in China. We may even be tempted to dismiss his theory as disorganized and rambling. However, a more thorough examination reveals an entirely different picture. We see a knowledgable man speaking about the importance of drama as a literary genre, the unique qualifications of a playwright, the consequences of the concept that a play is to be performed on a stage, the choice of subject matter and themes, plot development, characterization and language, the use of dialogue, and the introduction of comic elements. Moreover, he also addresses himself to many of the problems associated with the production of plays and the training of actors. We shall discuss his ideas in each of the above-mentioned areas.

IV *Playwriting*

A *Drama as a Literary Genre*

Until very recently, actors and actresses had always been held in scorn by Chinese society. In fact, at one time offspring of actors and actresses were not allowed to participate in the state examinations and were forbidden to marry outside of their "caste."[12] If the acting profession was considered much less than honorable, not much more distinction and prestige were accorded playwrights. Most of the Yüan playwrights used pseudonyms. Only a few of them received any favorable recognition by society, and "most of them were humble literary craftsmen."[13] The Ming playwrights considered drama primarily a literary exercise and a diversion, and few took it seriously. Recognizing the social stigma attached to playwrights, Li Yü points out the importance of their writing:

Critics have considered playwriting as the least important skill, yet it still ranks higher than horse racing, sword-playing, wine-drinking or gambling. . . . I say a skill is judged by one's proficiency in it, and not by the nature of its importance. . . . The writing of *tz'u* poems which bears some relationship to our drama not only has made writers famous, but it has also absorbed the attention of emperors, and because of their talent in this literary genre their names and statecraft have been remembered by posterity. For example, writers like Kao Tse-ch'eng and Wang Shih-fu were noted scholars of Yüan, but their fame lies primarily in their plays. Had not they composed *The Story of the P'i-pa* and *The Western Chamber*, who would remember them today? . . . T'ang Hsien-tsu, a genius of the Ming period, is noted for his poetry, essays, and correspondence, but his fame today rests not with those works, but with his play, *Return of the Soul*. Each dynasty has been outstanding in one particular type of literature: Han for historical works as represented by the *Shih-chi* and the *Han-shu*, T'ang for poetry, Sung for prose, and Yüan for drama. Were it not for the production of numerous plays including the *P'i-pa* and *The Western Chamber*, the memory of the Mongol Yüan would have faded and, like that of the Kitan and Jurchen Tartars, nothing would be left worth remembering. Therefore, the art of playwriting is not a minor skill but ranks in importance with writing history, biography, poetry and prose.[14]

B *The Playwright*

In addition to recognizing the importance of drama as an important literary genre, Li feels that a good playwright must have distinct qualifications. He must be knowledgable and well read in the classics and their commentaries, in philosophical works, history, poetry, parallel prose, in the works of Taoism, Buddhism, and other schools of philosophical thought, in the technical texts of all types of occupations, and be familiar even with such primers as *The Thousand Character Classic* and *The Hundred Names*.[15]

In addition to a sound scholastic background, Li feels that a good playwright needs to have a flexible mind and the ability to assume the role of each of the characters he describes. If he wants to describe a virtuous character, he must be able to think as one; on the other hand, if he wants to portray a wicked and depraved character, he must temporarily give up his own way of thinking and adopt the mental processes of a wicked man.[16]

Perhaps the most formidable challenge to a playwright is his ability to handle "emotion" (*ch'ing*) and "scene" (*ching*) in his works. First, Li Yü makes a distinction between emotion and scene. Emotion is what is felt in each character's heart, whereas scene is what is observed by everyone and is derived from the external world. Obviously, Li feels that it is much more difficult to describe emotion than scene, as he says:

Emotion comes from one's mind, but scene is an observation of the external world. It is easy to depict a scene, but it is difficult to describe one's emotions. These two things are widely separated like heaven and earth. The former is unique with each person. The words used in describing Chang San [Tom] can never be applied to Li Ssu [Dick], whereas the scene is common to both. For example, in describing spring and summer, a playwright needs only to distinguish them from autumn and winter. A skillful playwright has to put more work on conveying emotion and less on describing the scene. Those who excel in writing about the scenes of visiting rivers and hills, on describing moonlight parties and appreciating flowers will only succeed partially if they cannot handle equally well their characters' emotions.[17]

In sum, Li does not believe that everyone can be a playwright; in fact, only those with born talents should try. And he suggests the following method of testing one's suitability for the profession: "If his conversation is not pedantic, he will show his inventiveness in one or two sentences out of ten; if his writing is not woodenly dull, he will reveal a lightness of touch in one or two paragraphs out of an essay. If he also shows imaginativeness, then he is suited for playwriting."[18] Li stresses innate gifts rather than hard work and diligence. As he eloquently puts it: "That which is acquired through hard work is usually second class."[19]

After duly emphasizing the importance of drama as a literary genre and the special qualifications of a playwright, Li laments that little is known about drama as an art. He cites the reasons for this as being (1) a lack of definite rules and (2) the selfishness and unwillingness of successful playwrights to share their knowledge with others. He feels it is his duty to make his knowledge of drama available to anyone who might be interested.[20]

C Drama is to be Performed on a Stage

Throughout much of Chinese history, the Chinese audience usually went to the theater to listen to fine music and embellished lyrics. Sometimes they just went to hear and see their favorite actor or actress perform the incredible feat of singing forty to fifty arias.[21] Few actors and still fewer members of the audience understood what the arias were about, and even fewer playwrights cared to correct this situation. They went on writing fine lyrics without any regard either for the actors or the audience. Perhaps this grave error resulted from their ignorance rather than from a deliberate effort to bedazzle the audience. This unfortunate situation was very common during Li's time, and he wanted intensely to draw the attention of other playwrights to it: "All in all, drama is not the same as other literary genres which are meant exclusively for the literate class. As such they are justified in being a little abstruse. Drama is meant to be performed before the literate and the educated as well as before the illiterate and uneducated women and children. Therefore, immediate comprehensibility is much preferable to intellectual challenge."[22]

It is only when the audience understands the play that the common theatrical experience can be shared by all, Li Yü maintains. In short, Li was one of the very few, if not the only, Chinese playwright who understood that "A play is to be performed on a stage before an audience. That audience is a group of people collected together in the same place and at the same time for the purpose of sharing the experience of the theater."[23]

D Subject Matter

Playwrights not only wrote long and unintelligible lyrics; many also showed a lack of originality. Li felt that many of the so-called contemporary plays were "not new at all but the patched frock of an old monk or a medicinal concoction put together by doctors, the plots taken from different old plays, one from here, and another from somewhere else."[24] And if there was any originality, it was usually in the wrong direction. Many of Li's contemporaries used supernatural, ridiculous, or exotic themes to dazzle the audience, or else they complained about the lack of usable themes.

The pleasure of attending a new play, Li says, is to hear what one has never heard before. He therefore considers originality and novelty in the subject matter as a means of securing the attention of the audience. A playwright should search for inspiration in normal human situations and not have to enter the realm of fantasy. Li reasons: "All plays which expound on human feelings and on natural laws will be appreciated from one generation to another, while those which are frivolous, incredible, ridiculous, and strange will be forgotten within the lifetime of the playwright. Which one of the Five Classics, the Four Books, the *Tso Commentary on the Ch'un-ch'iu*, the *Chan-kuo ts'e*, and the writings of the T'ang and Sung authors does not touch upon normal human activities?"[25]

As for the lack of usable material, Li explains: "Any material unused by writers of the past can be used. Even familiar stories already used by them may not have been fully exploited. If we put ourselves in the shoes of earlier writers and by entering into their stories comprehend the subtleties of the human emotions and the niceties of the human actions they describe, the deceased authors would inspire us with a lively pen, enabling us to write in a fresh and exquisite language. Then the audience will be so absorbed by the craft of the playwright as to forget that the story is an old and familiar one!"[26]

Furthermore, Li claims that a playwright can use familiar themes and yet produce surprisingly new results:

It was said that the day-to-day happenings have been exhausted by writers of the past and that even the most minute and extremely obscure incidents have been fully explored. That is why contemporary writers are looking for what is strange and bizarre. But I think this is not true. Not many extraordinary events happen in a humdrum world. The principles governing human emotions are infinite. As long as the relationships between rulers and officials, fathers and sons exist for one day, there will always be feelings and concepts of loyalty, filial piety, chastity, and righteousness. Human nature manifests itself in novel ways with the passing of time. There are certainly events of the past left for writers of a later generation to explore and to describe more sensitively, thus improving on what has been done by one's predecessors.[27]

To Li, a playwright has sufficient freedom in exploring the many intricate facets of human behavior without resorting to materials of a ridiculous nature. A playwright should strive for originality in human situations and emphasize themes true to the human condition such as separation, family reunion, tragedy, and happiness. These are themes that have the power to make people cry, laugh, be happy or angry, as well as to arouse in the audience feelings of sympathy and suffering.

The ability to be creative and original within the confines of familiar themes is a most important asset to a playwright, and he can never fully exhaust the infinite varieties of human behavior. Moreover, a paywright must never be too specific. In extolling the virtues of filial piety, a playwright needs to cite the example of only one filial son and only one of his deeds, and it need not be historical in nature, because drama is no more than a reflection of life. In fact, a playwright has a unique opportunity to fabricate stories as long as they are plausible.[28] Though a playwright has considerable freedom in exercising his imaginative powers, he must never forget that "the origin of drama was to help ignorant men and women to be good, and to warn against evil deeds."[29]

E The Plot

Prior to Li's time, drama was rather weak in plot development. One of the reasons was that the Chinese audience went to the theater to see their favorite actors singing and performing familiar roles in familiar stories. Precisely because of the audience's blind acceptance of plays with weak plots, no critic before Li had spoken intelligently of the importance of plot development in drama.[30] Consequently, few playwrights had any idea or concept of the need for unity in a plot, and many playwrights after the Yüan period often "placed their emphasis on the branches and leaves of a play instead of on its root and trunk. They thought that an additional character would bring about more side issues, so that the audience would feel like one lost in a maze, completely dazzled."[31] Li did his best to point out the errors of this approach and suggested a "one-person-one-event" formula: "Apart from the protagonist who is the primary concern of the playwright, all other characters are secondary. All the partings and unions, joys and sorrows that befall the protagonist are there to illuminate the significance of one major event to him. This one-person-one-event formula constitutes the 'brain' of the play."[32] He cites the example of *The Story of the P'i-pa* in which the protagonist is Ts'ai Po-chieh and the main event is his remarriage into the Niu family. All the complications arise from this event. In other words, Ts'ai's remarriage is the "brain" of the play.[33]

In addition to establishing the concept of the "brain" of a play, Li goes on to say that an effective play must appear probable and convincing to the audience. In criticizing *The Story of the P'i-pa*, Li asks: "How is it possible for Ts'ai Po-chieh's family not to have heard about his success in the imperial examination after three long years? Couldn't Ts'ai have sent word to his family? Second, Chao Wu-niang journeyed more than one thousand *li* in search of her husband. Could she have remained undefiled during that long journey? Who can vouch for her chastity?"[34]

Furthermore, a playwright needs to provide a tight texture for his play. In Li's view, a dramatic composition is similar to fine needlework: "The entire cloth is first cut into pieces and sewn in a pattern. The art of integration lies in the tightness of the texture of the needlework, since one careless stitch will render the whole piece imperfect."[35] Therefore, in composing a scene, a playwright must consider what went before and what will follow: "The previous scenes serve to point to and foretell the present one, while the subsequent scenes serve to echo, to recall, and to suggest." Furthermore, he must have the overall structure of the play constantly in mind, including all the characters to be presented and all the related incidents.[36] The end result should be a well-constructed play with no signs of disjointedness. Like the blood vessels of an organism, the play should flow smoothly from beginning to end with any seemingly unrelated parts contributing to the ultimate unity of the plot.[37] To achieve this, a playwright must use his judgment. In short, what Li Yü suggests is quite similar to what Gustave Freytag (1816–1895) said in *Techniques of the Drama* (1863): "It is the business of the action to represent to us the inner consistency of the event, as it corresponds to the demands of the intellect and the heart. Whatever, in the crude material, does not serve this purpose the poet is in duty bound to throw away."[38]

Where Freytag speaks of five component parts of a dramatic play—(1) introduction, (2) rise, (3) climax, (4) return or fall, and (5) catastrophe or denouement[39]—Li offers the prologue (*chia-men*), the small roundup (*hsiao shou-sha*), and the big roundup (*ta shou-sha*). We may equate Li's prologue with Freytag's introduction and rise; the small roundup with the climax and return; and the big roundup with the catastrophe.

Li sees the prologue as a most vital part of any play: "The first few words of a play are called the prologue [*chia-men*]. The words may be brief, yet they cannot be satisfactorily phrased unless the playwright has an idea of the overall structure of the play."[40] Immediately following the prologue comes the second scene (*ch'ung-ch'ang*), the purpose of which is to introduce the main characters. And Li considers this scene vital in determining the success or failure of a play.[41] Of equal importance to the expert handling of the second scene is the order of appearance of the characters. Li insists that the important characters not be introduced too late in the play; otherwise, the audience might view those who preceded them as the major ones and regard them as only secondary.[42]

In Western drama there are the rising movement and the climax. The climax is the place where the results of the rising movement come out strongly and decisively. Likewise, Li maintains that toward the end of the first half of the play no new characters should be introduced and that the suspense should be maintained, giving the audience an opportunity to guess at what will follow. He calls this part the small roundup.

Equivalent to Freytag's catastrophe is the big roundup, a scene that Li considers to be most challenging to write. He explains why: "The important characters, numbering about five in number and having been scattered in various directions throughout the play, must now be brought together in the concluding scene."[43] But unfortunately, many inept playwrights simply bring all the characters together without providing the audience with any logical reason for this. Consequently, they only succeed in antagonizing the audience, giving it the idea that the denouement has been a deliberate contrivance on the part of the playwright rather than a logical development. A good concluding scene, in Li's view, is to have all the characters come together, very much like water flowing naturally and smoothly into a pool.[44]

In short, a successful play has a "brain" (that is, a focus), a tightly knit structure, a good prologue, elements of suspense, and a logical and convincing conclusion, while at the same time a playwright must entertain his audience with elements of unpredictability or surprise within the vast world of the many different facets of human emotions and feelings.[45]

F *Characterization and Language*

Western drama presents characterization through action and dialogue, whereas Chinese drama, with its traditional emphasis on music and singing, characterizes through language, an area in which Li has made many contributions. First, to present convincing characters Li thinks a playwright must be careful in his choice of words. He explains: "Language is the expression of the feelings of the heart. If a playwright is to speak for a character, he must first show the feelings of the character he is going to portray."[46] Thus a virtuous character should speak like one and a wicked character should use a language revealing the evil thoughts he possesses. What Li abhors is a character who uses language inappropriate to his role, such as a male lead character (*sheng*) using the language of a clown or vice versa. And he firmly believes that language is vital to character delineation.

And that language must be simple, for as Li says: "If a play has to be thought about and pondered over before it can be understood, it cannot be considered a drama of high quality."[47] Moreover, he sees the language of drama as distinctly different from that of poetry: "The value of poetry is in its refinement and elegance; crudity and vulgarity are condemned. So its language has to convey the meaning explicitly. Dramatic language [or the language in a play] is different. Its dialogue is based on the living language of ordinary people and the plot is taken from everyday life."[48] While he emphasizes a simple language, he does not condone crude or vulgar language.

Among the many common errors Li condemns in the writing of plays are pedantry and padding: "The tricks commonly used to pad out a work are three: profuse allusions to past events, constant mention or use of names of historical figures, and the wholesale borrowing of quotations. The reasons for such practices also number three: to show off one's learning, to achieve felicity of expression in disguised artificiality, and to use ready-made substitutes for originality of thought."[49]

Deploring bookishness in contemporary plays, Li expresses his admiration for the simplicity of Yüan drama:

It is not that the Yüan dramatists did not have solid academic backgrounds. It is simply that they did not make use of their academic knowledge, whereas the songs of contemporary playwrights are filled with purposefully conspicuous erudition. Yüan playwrights did not lack depth, although their songs may appear to be simple. They aimed at depth in simplicity. And even if the songs are simple, it does not mean that the plays lack depth. But the songs of contemporary playwrights are simple neither in meaning nor in language.[50]

Horace once said: "It is not enough for poems to be fine; they must charm and draw the mind of the listener at will."[51] Similarly, Li speaks of the importance of organic unity and wit in drama in charming and drawing the attention of the audience:

Organic unity and wit are two indispensable qualities in drama. The former is the internal spirit of drama, while the latter is its external manifestation. If these two are wanting, the play is like a clay man or a clay horse: only the shape of a living form without any breathing spirit—clearly the result of a playwright's inferior craftsmanship. Such a playwright pads out his work sentence by sentence, forcing his audience to remember the play section by section. If the audience becomes only slightly inattentive, it will not be able to recall what the previous song or scene was about. When watching the second act, it will have no idea of what is likely to be forthcoming in the next. If a play is written in such a disjointed manner, it will only make the eyes and ears of the audience sore.[52]

G Dialogue

Every Yüan play has poetic songs (ch'ü) in various lyric meters as well as prose passages (pin-pai). While the main characters express their emotions and feelings in poetic songs, the action of a play is carried by the prose passages.[53] Despite the importance of the dialogue to the overall effect of a play, it was generally poor in quality and its words unbefitting the pens of literary men. A statement in the Miscellaneous Comments on the Rules and Regulations of Drama (Ch'ü-lü tsa-lun) pinpoints the problem: "The Yüan drama songs are excellent but the dialogue is vulgar. . . . The reason is that the dialogue was composed by musicians and the playwrights were ashamed to make corrections. Hence in most cases the words in the dialogue do not make sense."[54] Worse yet, in some of the variety plays produced during the Ming period, the dialogue, created by the musicians instead of the playwrights, was not even included. Such a glaring shortcoming was noted by some of the more sophisticated critics. Wang Chi-te said that the dialogue in a play should be clear and concise, and that words with level and oblique tones should be used equally. Another critic, Tsang Mou-hsün, pointed out in his preface to the *Selections from the Yüan Drama* that "In the twenty-one acts of *The Western Chamber*, there are few lines of dialogue,"[55] a lack he believed was due to the set rules of the dramatic tradition.

Li, of course, noticed such problems and their seriousness. He said:

It has been an established practice that only the language of the singing part is emphasized while that of the dialogue is neglected. I am often surprised to find songs as beautiful as the proverbial snow in spring existing side by side in the same play with dialogue as crude as the proverbial uncouth rustic. The reason is probably that in the Yüan drama the playwrights of the variety plays were mainly writing Northern-type songs and concerned themselves only with the singing parts while the spoken parts may have been later interpolations. Since the spoken part was not what the Yüan playwrights emphasized, only slight attention was paid to it.[56]

To redress the problem, Li declared most unequivocally that "the importance of dialogue to a play is analogous to the commentaries vis-à-vis the classics, the pillars vis-à-vis the small rafters in construction, and to having blood in one's body."[57] And it is certainly true to say that Li made significant contributions in this area, as he unabashedly declared: "The complexities of dialogue in drama began with me. While some critics have praised me for it, others have condemned me. Although many playwrights assumed that no specific attention need be given to it, I have always insisted that every word of dialogue must be hammered out with extraordinary care."[58] Furthermore, he says that the "most satisfying songs should be accompanied by equally successful dialogue. When both songs and dialogue are full of the living spirit of the writer, they enliven each other. Very often, a line of well-written dialogue can conjure up endless feelings in the songs."[59]

To help playwrights achieve the desired effects in writing their dialogue, Li suggests that they use clear and ringing words to stimulate the interest of a bored and tired audience, that they use appropriate language befitting the station of every character, that they drastically delete inessentials after a script has been completed, that they do not confuse words of Southern and Northern origins, that they economize on words, that they use an exquisite style, that they restrict the use of dialects, and that they pay attention to possible inconsistencies.

As for possible inconsistencies, Li cites the example of Ch'en Miao-ch'ang in the play *The Jade Pin*, in which there is a reference to Ch'en sitting in contemplation in a *ch'an-t'ang* ("a room in a Buddhist monastery") dressed in a black robe. Both *ch'an-t'ang* and "dressed in a black robe" are Buddhist expressions, most unsuitable to be used with regard to Ch'en who is a Taoist nun.[60]

To test the appropriateness of every line of dialogue, Li further suggests that a playwright put himself in the position of each character he describes, as Li himself claims to have done so in writing his plays.

There is no doubt that Li drew the attention of other playwrights to this area of criticism in the writing of plays. Not only did he draw others' attention to it, he was also the first critic to offer comprehensive commentaries on the subject. On one occasion, through the mouth of one of his friends, he neatly summed up his own contributions to the art of writing dialogue: "Speech in drama, as a rule, has been treated merely as words casually uttered, whereas Li Li-weng regards its composition with the same reverence with which he ponders the choice of a word in producing a literary composition."[61]

H *Comic Elements*

During Li's time, plays were staged either in the daytime or at night; the excessive length of many of them quickly bored the audience and put many to sleep. To combat the monster of sleep, Li suggests that attention be paid to the introduction of comic jests which should be natural and not contrived, humorous and yet instructive. The best comic jests, in his view, are those bordering on being common but not to the extent of being base or gross. If they are not of a common nature, they tend to appear pedantic; but if they are too vulgar, they don't seem to have come from the pens of literary writers. Li names the *Return of the Soul*, one of the four famous plays entitled *The Four Dreams* by T'ang Hsien-tsu, as an example of a play embodying appropriate comic jests.[62] And he sternly warns against the introduction of obscene expressions or ribaldry on the stage. He explains:

The comic jests of the clowns [those with painted faces] in a play often border on the licentious and bawdy. Improper vulgarities, unmentionable even in the bedchamber, are sometimes publicly uttered on the stage, making those with good taste and virtue want to close their eyes and cover their ears. With an audience possibly consisting of both sexes, immoral words can only promote indecency. This is why immoral music and poems were to be banned in the state of Cheng in ancient times. However, we must not forget that the primary purpose of comic jests is to induce laughter. Since there are so many things in the world which make good butts for jokes, I can't see the reason why playwrights are so keen on the subject of sex.[63]

V *Production of Plays*

"The only reason for writing a play is to have it staged, and success or failure depends on many factors,"[64] declared Li Yü. He then proceeds to explain the fundamental factors contributing to the success of a play. First, a producer must choose wisely the plays to be staged. If he chooses a poor one, all his efforts and those of his actors will have been wasted.[65] Instead of selecting a play of noisy and exciting action, Li counsels that a play be chosen for its intrinsic dramatic qualities, which, to him, means one reflecting human nature. And such a play will be much more effective than one depending on simulated wars on the stage and thunderous drums in the orchestra. For these not only fail to move an audience but the earsplitting noise drives it away.[66]

Second, a producer must understand the psychology of his audience and stage his plays at night rather than during the day. Li is quite correct in observing that the stage, at best, offers an illusion of life, and the best time for providing such an illusion is at night when the surroundings are correspondingly dark. Moreover, Li feels that members of the audience must have other business to attend to during the day, and that they will feel more relaxed at night.[67]

Third, a producer must be prepared for all contingencies. When he has a captive and leisurely audience, he may have a play performed from beginning to end. On the other hand, if he has a less-than-attentive audience, he must be prepared to instruct his actors to delete the less exciting parts, even altering some of the dialogue, retaining only the most important.[68]

Fourth, a producer must also serve as an editor. In staging old plays, he must delete parts which seem unlikely or contradictory in terms of human behavior. He must be equally good in patching flaws found in the original work.[69]

Fifth, a producer should also pay attention to the musical accompaniment. When it is played too loudly, it frequently drowns out the singing of the actors: "The stringed instruments, the bamboo instruments, and the human vocal chords were employed independently in the past. They have been used together only very recently. It is desirable to hear these three sounds in combination. But the voice should have the dominant or leading part, with the stringed and bamboo instruments subordinated, so that even what is not naturally produced approaches most closely the natural way of producing music, that is, singing."[70] Furthermore, if the gongs and the drums are played at the wrong time, they can destroy the play and its performance. For example, great damage can be done when the gongs and drums unwarrantedly interrupt a speech that is not finished or a song that has just started. For these reasons, Li warns that a producer must make sure that the rhythm of songs and drums are kept in complete harmony.[71]

Sixth, a producer should also pay attention to theatrical errors in costuming, to the extensive freedom allowed clowns and their indiscriminate use of the Wu (Soochow) dialect, to the excessive use of exclamatory words such as *Ya* and clichés such as *Ch'ieh-chu* ("wait a minute"), and to unseemly horseplay on the stage.[72]

Li also felt most strongly that the rich and the influential had to bear the major responsibility for quality stage performances. As patrons of the theater, they had unlimited influence on the profession and should insist on quality. He says: "At present the theater is drowned out by thunderous cacophony, and melodies of high quality have long been silent. It is neither because singers were born at the wrong time nor because actors were badly directed by their teachers. The fault actually lies with the audience. Were there only a few among those holding important posts who would boycott such feelingless performance or who would not provide them even when they are requested at a party, or who would boo them before they are finished. . . . If the audience would demand quality, the actors would not dare stage plays negligently."[73]

VI   *The Training of Actors*

Since the establishment of the Pear Garden during the T'ang dynasty, musicians, actors, and dancers had been trained to perform at imperial banquets and other festival occasions. Such training was continued during the Sung and Yüan dynasties, its emphasis primarily on recitation and singing. Most actors came from poor families and were illiterate, and difficult as it is to believe, they had no idea of the meaning of the songs they sang. Sometimes they wore happy expressions on their faces when they were singing about tragic events and vice versa, or else they mumbled their words so indistinctly that they bored their audiences.[74]

As singing was the most important part of Chinese drama, Li felt that the training of actors must begin with the teaching of singing. A teacher should first explain the meaning of each song to his students, because "the trick of vitalizing a stale libretto into a lively song and transforming an artisan into an artist lies entirely in the understanding of the song. This understanding is indeed of utmost importance."[75]

Then the teacher should teach his students the proper pronunciation of words. Again the reasons are self-evident. Li says: "A student of singing, whether or not he is talented, must see to it that he is 'heard.' An audience will first have to be able to distinguish the words of a song before it can consider the quality of the singing."[76] Therefore, Li stresses, it appears advisable for an apprentice-actor to aim at clarity of diction as his first goal and to exercise his vocal cords in such a way that every word is distinct.[77]

Once an actor is able to pronounce clearly the initial, final, and remanent sounds of a word, he may be taught to sing with his heart rather than just with his mouth:

When a song is sung only with the mouth and not from the heart, or when it is only a matter of the vocal organs without any facial expressions or bodily response, it is an expressionless song. It will be as forced and unnatural as the humdrum recitation of a village-school child. Even though the singing technicalities [that is, the tunes and the maintenance of the beat or tempo with a pair of castanets] may be accurate and the pronunciation of words absolutely clear, such a song remains second-rate or worse, falling far short of the highest quality.[78]

The foregoing principles of singing can also be profitably applied to the spoken parts, though Li believes that it is much more difficult to master elocution than the art of singing. He explains why:

In singing, the modulation of rise and fall, the tempo of quick and slow are governed by regulations, all explicitly written down in the musical scores and strictly taught by the teacher. Once an actor gets used to it through training, he will then naturally follow the right way. But in elocution, the modulation of rise and fall and the regulation of tempo have neither formulated rules nor are they indicated as in musical scores, and everything depends on the instruction of the teacher.[79]

Most definitely, elocution is an art. An actor must inflect his voice, and change pitch and tone in order to communicate the exact sense expressed in the lines. Variations in pitch, volume, and timing constitute the rhythm of speech, the mastery of which is what Li wishes all actors to acquire:

The speech of a play is just ordinary speech, but there are principles governing its delivery. . . . We know that speech varies in pitch and cadence. As to when it should be high and rising or low and falling, the answer is the same as that for singing. In a song, we can distinguish the primary from the secondary or padding words outside the melodic form [ch'en-tzu]. . . . In elocution the primary words will be spoken with a higher pitch and with more emphasis, while the secondary will be lower and more suppressed in tone. This is a correct and well-established rule as well as the most workable and simple approach in speech writing.[80]

In addition to variations in volume and pitch, the rate of speed in the delivery of words is important to an actor. Li describes its importance in metaphorical terms: "Varying the speed of speech is as essential to an actor as graceful elegance is to a lady's posture."[81] A uniform pace or a delivery that is too quick or too slow will either bore or irritate the audience. The pause is, therefore, vitally important to the speaker. Sometimes short pauses between words and sentences are more desirable than constant loquacity, for such pauses might put across the feelings of surprise or anticipation to the audience. In general, Li offers the following guidelines: "When two or three sentences deal with the same theme, they should be spoken in one breath without any long pauses in the middle. When the first sentence is about one thing and the next is about something else, or when there are divergences from a certain point, we should then pause at the end of the first before beginning the second."[82]

Besides stressing many aspects of the mastery of the art of singing and elocution, Li insists on natural and lively acting so that each character properly portrays his role, since the violation of any of the mannerisms associated with each particular character could destroy the total effect of a play.

VII *Conclusion*

Despite what Li has suggested in his book on many of the aspects of the theater, he feels that in his work he has not followed his own principles: "I have always been poor and to make a living I traveled nearly all year long. Whenever I wrote anything I usually had to finish it in a hurry. It is not that I did not want to make revisions, but I simply did not have the time. As soon as I completed a play, it was snatched away from me by the printers. . . ."[83] On another occasion he says: "Even if Heaven graces me with more years to live, so that I might be able to produce more plays in addition to the ten which have been staged, I wonder whether I could, like a cock crowing at dawn, say all that is in my mind."[84]

In conclusion, though there are critical works on drama prior to Li's time, none emphasized structure as well as prosodic, rhetorical, and musical details.[85] His comprehensive theory stemmed from his own experiences in the theater and from what he observed of the works of his predecessors, much like Aristotle, who formulated his theory by evaluating the works of famous Greek dramatists. With complete candor and sincerity, Li pointed out the shortcomings of the Chinese stage and made constructive suggestions to correct them.

Perhaps it is not too much of an exaggeration to say that Li's dramatic theory, though firmly rooted in Chinese soil, transcends the confines of Chinese drama and offers enlightening comparisons with Western literary criticism. His idea of the need to express human feelings and present human nature in drama is much the same as Samuel Johnson's idea that nature and passion are the chief concerns of a poet. His views of emotion and scene in drama find an echo in T. S. Eliot's principle of "objective correlatives" in poetry. His thoughts on the edification of the audience through entertainment are similar to the concept of "instruction with delight" advocated by Ben Johnson, John Dryden, and other Restoration critics. And lastly, his discussions of dramatic construction not only bring to mind Gustave Freytag but also Aristotle's concept of the unity of action.[86]

Of the many contributions Li has made, none is more vitally important than his popularizing the concept that a play is to be staged before an audience—a group of people collected together in the same place and at the same time for the purpose of sharing the experience of the theater—and that every effort must be made by the playwright, the producer, and the actor to satisfy that audience. For this concept alone the Chinese theater is much indebted to him.

CHAPTER 7

Looking Backward

THOUGH born in an age which stressed conformity and cor-
rectness in personal conduct, Li Yü was a free and romantic
spirit. Early in life he abandoned his academic career to pursue one
in writing and the theater, and to discourse on the art of living.
Neither financial woes nor personal frustrations dampened his zest
for life or lessened his interest in his literary work. In *A Temporary
Lodge for My Leisure Thoughts* he pointed out that a life of happiness was possible at every socioeconomic level. Unlike Thoreau who
tried to reduce the necessities of life to a minimum, Li emphasized
doing the best one could with what one had with regard to clothing,
food, shelter, prevention of illness, and the regulation of one's sex
life. Using wit and metaphor, he marked out at least one road to a
good life.

He took his writing seriously. In addition to poetry and essays, he
wrote short stories, a novel of distinction, and ten plays, and he
edited many other works. As a storyteller, he distinguished himself
by using a simple and earthy style, creating characters all could
recognize, and by writing on subjects of interest and concern to the
average reader. In *Prayer Mat of Flesh,* he approached sexuality
with a sophisticated insight rarely found in a Chinese author; and in
his dramatic works and essays, he emerged as a comic genius and as
the foremost drama critic in the history of Chinese drama criticism.

He was well known among his contemporaries, so well known in
fact that even illiterate people had heard of him. His literary talent
impressed and fascinated his friends and the general public. But
many others condemned his entertainment-oriented writings, his
advocacy of the pursuit of happiness, his unorthodox way of earning
a livelihood, and his high style of living. One contemporary, Tung
Han, spoke of Li in the *San-kan chih-lüeh (chüan* 4) as follows:

Li Yü was mean, filthy, and dishonorable. He was obsequious and skillful in anticipating and meeting people's wishes. And he frequently had three or four country whores with him. Whenever he met young masters from noble or wealthy families, he would ask his girls to sing for them behind a screen or to drink with them. For the gain of fabulous profits, he discoursed on the art of love and, completely without scruples, induced his listeners to follow his advice. His behavior was so base that he was scorned by scholars. I met him once and have shunned him ever since.[1]

Such condemnation and attacks were reflected in later writings about him. For example, though Li had spent more than twenty years in Nanking and his last years in Hangchow, he is mentioned neither in the *Local Gazetteer of the District of Ch'ien-t'ang* (*Ch'ien-t'ang hsien-chih*, compiled in 1718), nor in the personalities section in the *Gazetteer of the Prefecture of Chiang-ning* (*Chiang-ning fu-chih*, compiled in 1790). Only a brief biography of Li (numbering fewer than sixty characters and written by Wang Ting-ch'ao) is included in the *Kuo-ch'ao ch'i-hsien lei-cheng* compiled by Li Huan: "Li Yü. His courtesy name, Li-weng, was a native of Ch'ien-t'ang. Lived in Nanking for many years. Author of *Sayings of One School* [*Yi-chia yen*] and some short stories in literary Chinese following the style of the T'ang authors. . . . He wrote ten plays including *Errors of the Kite* and edited the first, second, and third editions of the *Painting Patterns of the Mustard Seed Garden*."[2] Wang's account contains two important errors. First, Li was not a native of Ch'ien-t'ang (Hangchow), though he retired and died there. Second, Li's short stories were written in colloquial Chinese and bear no resemblance whatsoever to the famous T'ang *ch'uan-ch'i* stories.

In another sketchy account written by Liu T'ing-chi in the *Miscellaneous Records of the Tsai Garden* we find the following:

. . . Shen Yi-t'ang, the supervisor of instruction, once commented on Li as a scholar "more clever than erudite," a criticism fair and true. Wherever Li went, he brought with him a group of beautiful girls, either from Shensi or from Soochow, trained to sing enchantingly to the beat of red castanets. Sojourning in Peking at one time, Li inscribed three big characters saying "Home of [the] Lowly" on the gate to his hostel; someone else who disliked Li wrote three other characters meaning "Home of [the] Decent" on the opposite entrance. While Li was trying to be humble, the other was showing his disgust with Li's female companions. As a matter of fact, the rhyme book compiled by Li Yü is fairly good; his *Sayings of One School* containing many classical *tz'u* poems as well as articles on historical criticism prove that Li was a man of special insight.[3]

A more detailed but not really satisfactory biography of Li is contained in the *Gazetteer of the District of Lan-ch'i (Lan-ch'i hsien-chih)* compiled in 1888:

Li Yü, whose other name was Che-fan, was a native of Hsia-li village of this district. As a youth he qualified himself for the *hsiu-ts'ai* degree, and his writings on the Five Classics were highly appreciated by the regional examiner. Li was very well versed in classical poetry and prose, and was regarded as a talented man. He was fond of traveling. After moving to Hangchow from Nanking, he established himself in a neighborhood that included beautiful hills and the West Lake, and adopted the style name "Fisherman of the Lake." . . . He was clever in introducing a number of novel designs for the style and decoration of windows, furniture and curtains, dresses and ornamental objects, and domestic utensils, all of which were so attractive that they delighted many people. He was the friend of talented scholars and social dignitaries, and his name was known even to women and children. In his later years, he wished to return to Lan-ch'i and expressed a nostalgic longing in a piece of parallel prose entitled "Returning Home," in which he said that he would very much like "watching a cup of wine floating on the Ku stream [a river in Lan-ch'i] and making a garland entwined with orchids." Many of his literary writings are included in his *Sayings of One School*. In the prologue to his compilation *A New Book on Government Administration [Tzu-chih hsin-shu]*, he mentioned the advisability of handling judicial matters with extreme caution and of leniency in meting out penal sentences. His remarks show he was humane and compassionate. [These remarks have been included in *Huang-ch'ao ching-shih wen-p'ien* edited by Ho Ch'ang-ling or Ho Ou-keng, who mistook Li Yü for a native of the area south of the Yangtze.] Li was intelligent and quick in thought. Whenever he was asked to compose an essay on a particular subject, he would finish it while his guest was waiting for it at his house. Many of his writings, however, do not strictly follow the rules of rhetoric of ancient times. He excelled in the writing of drama; ten of his plays are known to all. In writing drama he did not imitate the works of his predecessors such as Kao Tse-ch'eng or Wang Shih-fu. During the last years of the Ming dynasty, Li Cho-wu [Li Chih, 1527–1602] and Ch'en Chung-ch'un, also known as Ch'en Mei-kung [1558–1639], were the two literary giants. When Li Yü's name is added to theirs, they form a triumvirate. Critics have maintained that Ch'en Chung-ch'un's taste was more elegant, and that Li Yü's was more of a popular nature. When Li Yü lived in the Hsia-yi village of this district, he started the construction of ditches around the village which were later completed. This waterwork still benefits the people of our district.[4]

Li Yü has had very little luck with modern Chinese literary historians. Lu Hsün gave him only a few lines in A Brief History of Chinese Fiction;[5] Liu Ta-chieh in A History of the Flourishing of Chinese Literature omitted all details of Li's life and only briefly referred to Li's A Temporary Lodge for My Leisure Thoughts and to his dramatic works;[6] and Cheng Chen-to in Illustrated History of Chinese Literature was primarily interested in Li's dramas.[7] Chou Tso-jen in his collected essays, K'u-chu tsa-chi, singled out only Li's A Temporary Lodge for praise.[8] Therefore, it is not surprising that histories of Chinese literature written in English, with the exception of Liu Wu-chi's An Introduction to Chinese Literature, have ignored him too.[9]

And despite the English, French, and German translations of some of his works in the late nineteenth and early twentieth centuries, there was no systematic evaluation of Li until the 1930s. Sun K'ai-ti was the first critic of note to hail Li as one of the most important Ch'ing short-story writers. With Sun breaking the ground in 1935, many Chinese and Western scholars since have been reevaluating Li's position in Chinese literature. Most notably, in 1959, Dr. Franz Kuhn considered Prayer Mat of Flesh a "significant novel which will surely live on in the literary history not only of China but of all civilized people."[10] In 1966, Dr. Helmut Martin completed a doctoral dissertation on Li's dramatic theory, Li-weng über Das Theater, followed by his expert editing of the Complete Works of Li Yü (Li Yü ch'üan-chi) in fifteen volumes. In 1974, Huang Li-chen published A Study of Li Yü (Li Yü yen-chiu) in Taipei. And, in 1975, the Chinese University of Hong Kong published a modern English rendition of Li's Twelve Towers, retold by Nathan Mao.

However impressive these recent developments have been, all important studies are either in German or in Chinese, and partial translations of Li's works can only provide a limited view of Li, the man and the writer. It has been the purpose of this study to present the highlights of his life and his manner of living; of his short stories and of *Prayer Mat of Flesh;* and an analysis of his dramatic theory. Hopefully, increased knowledge of the man and his works will bring him into the forefront of Chinese literature where he richly deserves to be.

Appendix 1

Textual Editions of Drama Without Sound (Wu-sheng hsi)

There are at least four different editions of the original *Drama Without Sound* and the relationships of one to the other are not altogether clear.[1]

(A) *The Second Collection of Drama Without Sound (Wu-sheng hsi erh-chi).*

(B) *The Combined Collection of Drama Without Sound (Wu-sheng hsi ho-chi).* Its heading reads: "Order of stories by Chüeh-shih pai-kuan (Li Yü) and commentaries by Shui-hsiang chi-chiu." Shui-hsiang chi-chiu was the pen name of Tu Chün (1611–1687), a good friend of Li Yü. Tu compiled the first and second collections of *Drama Without Sound* and titled it "The Combined Collection" *(ho-chi).* Mr. Ma Lien, or Ma Yü-ch'ing (d. 1935) of China had one incomplete copy, the only one known to be in existence. It contains only two stories and a preface by Tu Chün.[2]

(C) *The Complete Collection of Lien-ch'eng-pi (Lien-ch'eng pi ch'üan-chi).* This Japanese transcribed copy found in Dairen, China, has twelve stories with a supplement that lists six additional stories, the last two of which are missing. The title has been changed from *Wu-sheng hsi* to *Lien-ch'eng pi.* The translated titles of individual stories are as follows:

C1   "T'an Ch'u-yü Conveys His Love in a Play. Liu Miao-ku Dies Faithful to Her Lover"
C2   "An Old Astrologer Jestingly Changes the Horoscope. A *Yamen* Runner Becomes Rich"
C3   "A Beggar Does a Good Deed. The Emperor Plays Matchmaker"
C4   "An Honest Official Is Cleared of the False Rumor of Committing Incest With His Daughter-in-law. An Innocent Scholar Cannot Redress a Thieving Woman's Grievance"
C5   "Beautiful Women All Share Wedding Misfortunes. A Country Lad Uniquely Enjoys Bedroom Bliss"
C6   "Encountering Storms and Pirates, a Merchant Earns Marvelous Wealth. To Transfer and Return Venture's Capital to the Rightful Owner Makes Another Wealthy"
C7   "A Shrewish Wife Keeps Grass Widowhood. A Cowardly Husband Remarries His Wife"

141

C8   "A Wife and a Concubine Ruin the Proper Relations Between Husband and Wife. A Maid Fulfills the Requirements of Virtue and Chastity"
C9   "A Widow Schemes to Get a Mate. Several Beautiful Women Unite in Securing a Talented Scholar"
C10   "A Concubine's Jealousy Wrongs a Proper Wife. Old Relationships Are Restored to Prepare the Way for Family Harmony"
C11   "A Good Servant, Respectful of Righteousness and Loyalty, Arranges His Master's Burial. Foolish Descendants Coveting Wealth Lose Their Lives"
C12   "A Virtuous Woman, Upholding Her Virtue, Suffers from Slander. Jesting Among Friends Causes Unusual Wrongs"

Supplement:

S1   "Having Fallen into the Well of Catastrophe, a Woman's Wit Preserves Her Chastity. Saved From the Enemy's Mouth, She Clears Her Name and Spreads Her Fame"
S2   "By the Power of a Bodhisattva, a Man Asks for a Son and Gets a Daughter. The Heavens Are Moved to Change the Daughter Into a Son"
S3   "Arousing Public Ire, a Lover Loses His Life and His Boy-wife. Castrating Himself and Bringing Up the Orphan, the Survivor Repays His Lover's Memory"
S4   "A Son Falls Victim to a Gambler. Deceived by the Ghost of His Victim's Father, the Gambler Is Made Bankrupt"

(D) *Drama Without Sound* (*Wu-sheng hsi*) in twelve chapters. The copy in Sonkeikaku Library, Tokyo, was reprinted in Taipei in 1969. It contains twelve stories, with shorter titles which vary slightly in wording from those in *The Complete Collection of Lien-ch'eng pi* (*Lien-ch'eng pi ch'üan-chi*). They are the following:

D1   "An Ugly Bridegroom, Fearful of Beautiful Women, Is Uniquely Blessed With Them"
D2   "A Handsome Man, Trying to Avoid Sex Scandals, Manages to Create Them"
D3   "With the Change of His Horoscope, the Misery of a *Yamen* Runner Ends and His Happiness Begins"
D4   "Loss of Fortune, the Fruit of Disaster, Turns Out to be the Root of Happiness"
D5   "A Female Ch'en P'ing Plots Seven Schemes"
D6   "A Male Mother Meng Changes His Residence Three Times to Protect His Foster Child"
D7   "An Official, Patronizing a Prostitute, Hears the Complaint of Her Former Customer"
D8   "The Father's Ghost Wreaks Revenge for the Son's Gambling Debts"
D9   "By a Strange Bargain, a Bodhisattva Transforms a Daughter Into a Son"
D10   "Replacing the Concubine With the Wife Is the Marvelous Work of the Divine"

D11   "A Son and a Grandson Abandon the Ancestral Corpse and the Servant
           Arranges the Burial"
D12   "The Abandoned Wife and the Concubine Remarry and the Maidservant
           Becomes the Child's Mother"

A comparison of (C) and (D) reveals that the stories in the first group
exactly correspond to those in the second even though their titles are
slightly different:

D1   "An Ugly Bridegroom . . ."
D2   "A Handsome Man . . ."
D3   "With the Change of . . ."
D4   "Loss of Fortune . . ."
D5   "A Female Ch'en P'ing . . ."
D6   "A Male Mother Meng . . ."
D7   "An Official . . ."
D8   "The Father's Ghost . . ."
D9   "By a Strange Bargain . . ."
D10   "Replacing the Concubine . . ."
D11   "A Son and a Grandson . . ."
D12   "The Abandoned Wife . . ."

C5   "Beautiful Women All Share . . ."
C4   "An Honest Official . . ."
C2   "An Old Astrologer . . ."
C6   "Encountering Storms . . ."
S1   "Having Fallen Into . . ."
S3   "Arousing Public Ire . . ."
C3   "A Beggar Does a Good Deed . . ."
S4   "A Son Falls Victim . . ."
S2   "By the Power of a Bodhisattva . . ."
C10   "A Concubine's Jealousy . . ."
C11   "A Good Servant . . ."
C8   "A Wife and a Concubine . . ."

A further examination reveals that the following stories are not included
in the (D) copy:

C1   "T'an-ch'u-yü Conveys His Love in a Play. Liu Miao-ku Dies Faithful to
           Her Lover"
C7   "A Shrewish Wife Keeps Grass Widowhood. A Cowardly Husband Re-
           marries His Wife"
C9   "A Widow Schemes to Get a Mate. Several Beautiful Women Unite in
           Securing a Talented Scholar"
C12   "A Virtuous Woman, Upholding Her Virtue, Suffers from Slander. Jesting
           Among Friends Causes Unusual Wrongs"

Appendix 2

Miscellaneous Works

Censorship began early in China, originating at least with the first emperor of Ch'in, the Shih Huang-ti (r. 221–209 B.C.), who was known to have burned books and buried scholars alive. Stringent control of the literary world continued in one form or another throughout Chinese history, and was enforced with particular vigor under the Manchu emperor Ch'ien-lung (Aisin-gioro Hung-li) of the Ch'ing dynasty (r. 1736–1796). Ch'ien-lung, in L. C. Goodrich's view, was a despot: "For all the munificence of his gifts to literature, he stands accused before the bar of public opinion for his open interference with the independence of scholars of his day, for his deliberate falsification of history, for his malice towards a score of authors (several deceased long before) and their descendants, and for his repeated burning of hundreds of books, woodblocks of many of them included."[1] Among the hundreds of books destroyed were some of Li Yü's which are no longer extant today. One of these was Li's *A Brief Account of History, Ancient and Modern (Ku-chin shih-lüeh)* which appears on the *List of Prohibited Books To Be Destroyed.*

From information included in Li's works themselves, we know that his literary output was prodigious. Apart from the short stories and the novels discussed earlier, his miscellaneous writings may be classified in two categories, works he edited and ones he wrote:

I *Works Edited by Li*

A Complete Anthology of Letters Old and New (Ku-chin ch'ih-tu ta-ch'üan) published in 1688. A comprehensive anthology of letters written by renowned people, dating from the period of the Warring States (402-221 B.C.) through the Ming dynasty.

A First Anthology of Letters (Ch'ih-tu ch'u-cheng) in 12 *chüan*. Preface dated 1660. An anthology of letters by distinguished writers who were Li's contemporaries. (There is a copy in the Library of Congress.)

A Second Anthology of Letters (Ch'ih-tu erh-cheng). Publication date unknown.

144

The Best of Ming Tz'u Poems (Ming-tz'u hsüan-sheng). Li penned the preface to this work in 1678, saying that he had edited it to meet the demands
  of a public interested in *tz'u* poetry.[2]
A New Book on Government Administration (Tzu-chih hsin-shu). Two collections of short essays by different writers on subjects dealing with government administration and judicial matters. The first collection in fourteen *chüan* has prefaces dated 1663 and was issued in the same year; and
  the second in twenty *chüan*, was published in 1667.
An Anthology of Parallel Prose (Ssu-liu ch'u-cheng) in twenty *chüan* published in 1671.
A New Anthology of Parallel Prose (Hsin Ssu-liu ch'u-cheng) in twenty
  chüan was published in 1671. Mr. Shen Hsin-yu, Li Yü's son-in-law,
  edited this work at Li's request and classified its contents as follows:
  people and places of importance, literary pursuits, letters and comments
  submitted to emperors, ceremonies, birthdays, famous sayings, weddings, births, festival dinners, material objects, memorable deeds of
  chastity and virtue, inscriptions on grave tablets, mourning, death, leisure, partings, humor and jokes, romance, Buddhist and Taoist teach-
  ings. Each section is arranged by subject, complete with annotations. The
  bookcover explains that the work was the product of more than ten years
  of expert editing. On its frontispiece is the statement that "a sequel to this
  anthology will soon be ready."
Poetic Rhymes of Li-weng (Li-weng shih-yün) in five *chüan*. A dictionary of
  rhymes. Published in 1673 and in 1715.
Tz'u Rhymes of Li-weng (Li-weng tz'u-yün) in four *chüan*. Publication date
  unknown.
*A Combined Compilation of the Chronological Histories (Kang-chien hui-
  tsuan).* Publication date unknown.
An Anthology of Ming Poetry (Ming-shih lei-yüan). Publication date and
  other data unknown. Mentioned in *An Anthology of Parallel Prose.*
*An Anthology of Selected Essays of Different Dynasties (Lieh-ch'ao wen-
  hsüan).* Publication date and other data unknown. Cited in the foreword
  to *An Anthology of Parallel Prose.*
A Brief Account of History, Ancient and Modern (Ku-chin shih-lüeh). Publication date unknown. Destroyed during the reign of Emperor Ch'ien-
  lung.
Strange Happenings Old and New (Chin-ku ch'i-wen) in twelve *chüan*.
  Preface dated 1679. This book was originally compiled by Ch'en Pai-hua,
  but was edited and abridged by Li Yü. It is a work intended to further
  women's education.
*The Illustrated Edition of the Romance of Three Kingdoms (Hsiu-hsiang
  San-kuo-chih).* Publication date unknown. Published by Ts'eng-yüan.
*The First of the Four Strange Books, The Ancient Edition of the Romance of
  Three Kingdoms (Ssu-ta-ch'i-shu ti-yi-chung Ku-pen San-kuo-chih)* in

twenty-four *chüan* and one hundred and twenty *hui* (chapters). Published in 1679. In Sun K'ai-ti's *Bibliography of Chinese Popular Fiction* (pp. 37–38), Sun mentions two more editions which are very similar, if not completely identical to this one.

The Original Edition of the Painting Patterns of the Mustard Seed Garden (*Yüan-pan ch'u-yin Chieh-tzu-yüan hua-chuan*). Preface dated 1679. Reprinted by Yu-cheng Book Company (Yu-cheng shu-chü) of Shanghai. No date.

II *Nondramatic Works by Li*

A Collection of Early Poems (*T'iao-ling chi*). Number of *chüan* unknown. This collection consists of poems written before Li reached age thirty. The date of its publication is unknown and no copy is extant; it was, however, published during Li's lifetime.

A Collection of Tz'u Poems (*Nai-ko tz'u*) in four *chüan*. Author's own preface is dated 1678. The first and second *chüan* are lyrical *tz'u* poems (*hsiao-ling*) which have fewer than fifty-eight characters each; the third *chüan* contains poems of between fifty-nine and ninety characters each (*chung-tiao*); and the fourth contains poems of more than ninety characters each (*ch'ang-tiao*). The poems reveal glimpses of Li's personal and family life, and of his feelings on such occasions as the birthdays and deaths of and separations from relatives and friends.

On the Ancients (*Lun-ku*) in four *chüan*. Under the title of *Li-weng pieh-chi*, it appears in the *Complete Edition of Yi-chia yen* (*chüan* 9 and 10). It has two prefaces, dated 1664 and 1665 respectively, written by Wang Shih-yün and Yü Huai and includes Li's commentaries on historical episodes and personalities.

A Temporary Lodge for My Leisure Thoughts (*Hsien-ch'ing ou-chi*) in sixteen *chüan*. First published in 1671 in Nanking, this book remains his best known. The sixteen *chüan* are on the following topics: 1–3, drama; 4–5, production of plays; 6–7, the grooming of women; 8–9, interior house design; 10–11, domestic utensils; 12, diet; 13–14, gardening; 15–16, mental hygiene. This work is included in the *Complete Edition of Yi-chia yen* (see below) but was erroneously divided into six *chüan*, and the last character *chi* ("lodge") in the original title was mistaken for *chi* ("gather").

Sayings of One School (*Yi-chia yen*). In Li's own words: "This is a collection of my poems, essays, and other writings. Recent writers have indiscriminately used the word *chi* ['collection'] as the term for their work, so why did I choose a different title? Because my work is unique. It was not written in imitation of the styles of either ancient or modern writers."[3] The critic Sun K'ai-ti surmised that there were two different editions of the *Sayings*. The first, containing prose essays, miscellaneous items, and probably some poems, may have been published not later than late 1673.

The second included only poems, these having been written in both the classic and modern styles, and was probably published in 1678, with a preface by Ting P'eng.[4]

As a collection, *Sayings* includes poems on such topics as lanterns, varieties of vegetables, visits to Li's ancestral home, the crowing of cocks, on crabs, and on various fruits such as lichees, strawberries, Mandarin oranges, grapes, and pears. In addition, there are prose prefaces and epilogues to books, epitaphic obituaries, eulogies, biographies, essays on miscellaneous subjects, occasional odes, parallel couplets written on scrolls, poems, and letters. Of particular interest to scholars are his one hundred and nine letters which faithfully and vividly record major and minor events of his life. They range from letters to family members to notes to friends asking for financial aid, from self-evaluation of his writing talents to trivial transactions with neighbors.

The Complete Edition of Yi-chia yen (Yi-chia yen ch'üan-chi) published in 1730. This one volume contains four of Li Yü's books, *Sayings of One School, A Collection of Tz'u Poetry, On the Ancients,* and *A Temporary Lodge for My Leisure Thoughts.* In its preface an anonymous editor, who called himself the Master of the Mustard Seed Garden, noted:

Mr. Li-weng of the West Lake wrote many works during his life, the most famous of which are *Sayings of One School, A Collection of Tz'u Poetry, On the Ancients,* and *A Temporary Lodge for My Leisure Thoughts.* These works have enjoyed great popularity among their readers since they first appeared nearly a hundred years ago. But in the past they were published separately, and readers of each were able to gain only a partial knowledge of the author. This may be likened to ascending a nine-story pagoda, complete satisfaction only being obtained when one has reached the top. I have therefore assembled all four and issued them as one book to give the reader a more comprehensive picture of the author.[5]

III *Dramatic Works by Li*

Li Yü wrote at least ten plays, two of which, *Ordained by Heaven* and *Errors of the Kite,* are popular and delightful comedies, still loved by many theatergoers, although they are not as often staged as they used to be. It is probable that Li wrote more plays, but if he did, they are no longer extant; nonetheless, eight others have been attributed to him, all collected under the title *Eight Ch'uan-chi Plays (Ch'uan-chi pa-chung).* Sun K'ai-ti, following the views of Yao Hsieh in *Chin-yüeh k'ao-cheng,* believes that they were the works of Fan Hsi-che of Ch'ien-t'ang. The title page of the book is confusing in that it indicates that the plays had been read and approved (*yüeh-ting*) by Li.[6] Moreover, Li also revised some famous works of his predecessors, such as *The Story of the P'i-pa* by Kao Tse-ch'eng, *The Bright Pearl (Ming-chu chi)* by Lu Ts'ai, and the *Nan Hsi-hsiang* by Li Jih-hua.[7]

Calling himself "the old slave of drama," Li was extremely proud of his

achievements in playwriting. His excellence lies neither in prosodic
refinement nor in rhetorical flourishes but in the originality of his plots, the
avoidance of local dialects, and the extensive use of dramatic dialogue. As a
result, all his plays were easy to perform and were warmly welcomed by
audiences impressed by their novelty and comprehensibility.

His ten comedies are as follows:

Pitying the Fragrant Companion (Lien-hsiang-pan) in two *chüan* and
thirty-six scenes. Probably Li's first dramatic work and also known as *The
Fragrance of Beauties (Mei-jen hsiang)*, it was written when he moved
from Lan-ch'i to Hangchow. It contains good poetry and dialogue, and
describes the efforts of a wife in trying to find a concubine for her husband. Thematically, it is different from the traditional "scholar-and-
beauty" routine by emphasizing the attachment of two women to each
other and how they share the affections of one man without feeling jealous. Despite its strong lesbian undertones, Huang Li-chen surmises that
it could have been inspired by Li's admiration for his wife who seemed to
harbor no jealous feelings toward his many concubines.[8]

Errors of the Kite (Feng-cheng wu) in two *chüan* and thirty scenes. A
comedy of errors based on mistaken identities and the workings of mischievous fate, it contains witty dialogue and sustained suspense. It begins
with the hero's kite accidentally falling into the hands of an ugly duckling,
and ends with the hero marrying the beautiful girl, instead of the ugly
one with whom he has a love tryst.

The Destined Marriage (Yi-chung yüan) in two *chüan* and thirty scenes,
probably written while Li was in Hangchow. It is interesting to note that
this play has a preface written by Huang Yüan-chieh, a talented woman
who lived in the same city. Although based on historical personages, the
plot is pure invention: a series of intrigues and mistaken identities leading
to the eventual union of two talented painters with two equally talented
girls. Emphasizing the traditional "scholar-and-beauty" theme, the language is more refined though it contains many comic lines.

The Mirage (Sheng-chung lou) in two *chüan* and thirty scenes, written while
Li was in Hangchow. The main and subplots are based on two Yüan plays:
Liu Yi Delivering the Message (Liu Yi ch'uan-shu) and *The Boiling of the
Sea (Chang-sheng chu-hai)* by Chang Yu. It includes the incident of the
sea being boiled dry to force two dragon kings to give consent to their
daughters' marrying two human scholars.

Female Phoenixes Courting the Male (Huang-ch'iu-feng) in two *chüan* and
thirty scenes. Although the preface written by Tu Chün is undated, we
know that the play was written in 1666. Based on Li's story "A Widow
Schemes to Get a Mate. Several Women Unite in Securing a Talented
Scholar" included in the *Drama Without Sound*, the hero in the play is
overshadowed by three crafty women contending for him. Li's message is

to warn his audience against female jealousy leading to family discord and deceit.

Ordained by Heaven (Nai-ho t'ien) in two *chüan* and thirty scenes, a play considered by Liu Wu-chi to be "the most successful of Li Yü's comedies" with "a well-constructed and fast moving plot," combining "humor, irony, pathos, and fantasy."[9] The main plot is similar to that of "An Ugly Bridegroom, Fearful of Beautiful Women, Is Uniquely Blessed With Them" in *Drama Without Sound*. However, in the play the ugly man is transformed into a handsome youth who wins the hearts and minds of three women, while in the story, the ugly man remains ugly and wins only the women's toleration of him.

The Pair-eyed Fish (Pi-mu yü) in two *chüan* and thirty scenes. Unable to overcome the objections of the girl's family, a pair of lovers drown themselves at sea. The waves, impressed with their undying love for each other, transform them into pair-eyed fish (sole or flounder) and later restore them to human form so that they can be wed. The play has a preface (dated 1679) by a woman writer Wang Tuan-shu from Shao-hsing.

The Jade Hair-pin (Yü sao-t'ou) in two *chüan* and thirty scenes. A romantic comedy centering on two look-alike women and the loss of a jade hairpin, a token of love. It describes the Ming Emperor Wu-tsung's (r. 1506–1521) affection for a famous prostitute. This play was probably written in the spring of 1658, approximately one year after Li had settled in Nanking.

The Happy Reunion (Ch'iao t'uan-yüan) in two *chüan* and thirty-three scenes. Based on "Tower of My Birth" in *Twelve Towers*, it describes the union of a father with his long-lost son. This play has a preface written by a Shu-tao-jen (The Taoist Resembling a Stink Cedar) dated 1668.

Be Circumspect in Conjugal Relations (Shen luan-chiao) in two *chüan* and thirty-six scenes. It describes the fortunes of two courtesans and their lovers and their eventual marriage. Li Yü visited Sian, Shensi, in 1667 where he became acquainted with Kuo Ch'uan-fang, an assistant magistrate. Kuo wrote a preface to the play dated in the same year.

Notes and References

Chapter One

1. The name (*tzu*) that a Chinese takes upon reaching the age of twenty.
2. For Li Yü's life, see *Lan-ch'i hsien-chih* (1888) 5/41a, 8/59a; *Hang-chou fu-chih* (1922) 170/lb; *Chekiang Hsin-ch'eng hsien-chih* (1679) 15/10b; Sun K'ai-ti, "Li Li-weng yü *Shih-erh lou*," *Library Science Quarterly* (Peking) 9, nos. 3–4 (1935), 379–441; Arthur Hummel, ed., *Eminent Chinese of the Ch'ing Period* (Washington, D.C., 1943), I, 495–97; *Jou Pu Tuan (Prayer Mat of Flesh)*, tr. Richard Martin from Franz Kuhn's German version (New York, 1963), pp. 357–76; Helmut Martin, *Li Li-weng über Das Theater* (Heidelberg, 1966), pp. 219–65; Huang Li-chen, *Li Yü yen-chiu* (Taipei, 1974), pp. 4–24; and *Li Yü's Twelve Towers*, retold by Nathan Mao (Hong Kong, 1975), pp. xi–xiii. Sun K'ai-ti erroneously gave Li Yü's birthplace as Ju-kao, Kiangsu province. Li was actually born in Hsia-chih district, Hupeh province. See *Li Yü ch'üan-chi (Complete Works of Li Yü)*, ed. Helmut Martin (Taipei, 1973), I, 493; hereafter cited as *LYCC*. In a letter to a friend, Li Yü wrote: "Even though my ancestral home was in Chekiang province, I was born in Chih-kao . . ." Sun mistook Chih-kao, which was under the jurisdiction of Hsia-chih district, Hupeh province, as Ju-kao in Kiangsu province.
3. Sun K'ai-ti, p. 386.
4. *LYCC*, II, 844.
5. Ibid., III, 1484–85.
6. Ibid., II, 841.
7. Ibid., II, 844–45.
8. Ibid., VI, 2723–24.
9. Ibid., II, 842; also, III, 1195.
10. Ibid., II, 854.
11. Ibid., I, 465; II, 938; III, 1233–35, 1497; V, 2281.
12. Ibid., VI, 2648.
13. Ibid., II, 723.
14. Ibid., I, 265–66.
15. Ibid., II, 856–57.
16. Ibid., II, 982–83.

17. Ibid., VI, 2337–38.
18. Ibid., I, 221–22; II, 874–75, 877; III, 1131, 1210, 1413.
19. Ibid., II, 648–49.
20. Ibid., I, 271; II, 1013.
21. Ibid., II, 1032–42.
22. Ibid., I, 260–76; see Huang Li-chen, p. 20.
23. Ibid., II, 863.
24. Ibid., I, 418–20.
25. Ibid., I, 524–25.
26. Ibid., II, 988. The allusion "Han-tan" comes from a T'ang story called "Pillow" (*Chen-chung chi*). The story describes a meeting between a young man and an old Taoist in an inn: "Resting his head upon a pillow lent to him by a fellow traveler, the young man fell asleep and in a few minutes dreamed that he lived a long and varied life." Han-tan was the name of the city where the young man had come from. See E. D. Edwards, *Chinese Prose Literature of the T'ang Period* (London, 1938), I, 33.
27. *LYCC*, VI, 2697–98.
28. Ibid., V, 2262–63; translation by Lin Yutang in *My Country and My People* (New York, 1935), p. 327.
29. *LYCC*, VI, 2537; translation by Lin in *The Importance of Living* (New York, 1937), p. 43.
30. *LYCC*, VI, 2565–66.
31. Ibid., VI, 2583–84; *Living*, p. 255.
32. *LYCC*, VI, 2585–86; *Living*, p. 255.
33. *LYCC*, VI, 2742.
34. Huang Li-chen, pp. 7, 15, 23.
35. *LYCC*, VI, 2337.
36. Ibid., VI, 2333–34; translation by Lin in *Living*, pp. 268–69, with slight changes by the authors.
37. *LYCC*, VI, 2339; *Living*, p. 269.
38. *LYCC*, VI, 2341–44.
39. Ibid., VI, 2370–72; see also *Living*, p. 272.
40. *LYCC*, VI, 2368; *Living*, p. 271, with minor changes.
41. *LYCC*, VI, 2450–56, 2459; *Living*, p. 270.
42. *LYCC*, VI, 2738–39, 2741; see also Lin's *The Importance of Understanding* (Cleveland, 1960), pp. 262–63.
43. *LYCC*, VI, 2747–56.
44. Ibid., VI, 2705–7; see also *Understanding*, pp. 214–15.
45. *LYCC*, VI, 2708; *Understanding*, p. 216.
46. *LYCC*, VI, 2713–29.
47. Ibid., V, 2200–201.
48. Ibid., V, 2211–12; see Huang Li-chen, p. 111.
49. *LYCC*, V, 2214; see Huang, p. 112.
50. *LYCC*, V, 2216–23; see also *Understanding*, pp. 232–35.

51. *LYCC*, VI, 2766–67.
52. Ibid., VI, 2771–76.

Chapter Two

1. Nathan Mao, "The Tradition of Seduction in Chinese Literature," *Enquiry* 1, no. 3 (Autumn, 1967), 1–11.
2. See also *T'ai-p'ing yü-lan*, *chüan* 881, *Ssu-pu ts'ung-k'an* edition (Shanghai, 1935), p. 8a.
3. See E. D. Edwards, *Chinese Prose Literature*, I, 1–21; see also Lai Ming, *A History of Chinese Literature* (New York, 1964), p. 190.
4. Lai Ming, p. 189.
5. Ibid., pp. 255–56. For the meaning of *pien-wen*, see A. Waley, *Ballads and Stories from Tun-huang* (London, 1950), pp. 244–45; Liu Ts'un-yan, *Buddhist and Taoist Influences on Chinese Novels* (Wiesbaden, 1962), I, 237.
6. J. Průšek, "Urban Centers: The Cradle of Popular Fiction," in *Studies of Chinese Literary Genres*, ed. C. Birch (Berkeley, 1974), p. 261.
7. Ibid., p. 265.
8. Lai Ming, pp. 270, 272. See also Patrick Hanan, *The Chinese Short Story* (Cambridge, Mass., 1973). For a special study of the *San-yen*, see J. L. Bishop, *The Colloquial Short Story in China* (Cambridge, Mass., 1956); for the *Erh-p'o* see *L'Amour de la Renarde*, trans. André Lévy (Paris, 1970).
9. John L. Bishop, "Limitations of Chinese Fiction" in *Studies in Chinese Literature*, ed. J. L. Bishop (Cambridge, Mass., 1965), p. 242.
10. *LYCC*, I, 418.
11. Sun K'ai-ti, "Li Li-weng yü *Shih-erh lou*," p. 440.
12. Ibid., pp. 427, 434, 424.
13. Ibid., p. 424.
14. Ibid., p. 435.
15. R. H. Van Gulik, *Sexual Life in Ancient China* (Leiden, 1961), pp. 107–8.
16. T'ung-tsu Ch'ü, *Law and Society in Ancient China* (Paris, 1961), p. 170.
17. Ibid., p. 172.
18. Ibid., p. 177.
19. Ibid., p. 183.
20. *LYCC*, XII, 5166.
21. Ibid., XII, 5174.
22. Ch'en P'ing died in 178 B.C. A great political schemer, he helped the founder of the Han dynasty with his Six Wonderful Plans. For details, see *Shih-chi*, *chüan* 56.
23. *LYCC*, XII, 5355–56.
24. Ibid., XII, 5359–60.
25. Ibid., XII, 5360–62.

154 LI YÜ

26. Ibid., XII, 5370.
27. Ibid., XII, 5375.
28. Quoted in Lien-sheng Yang's "The Concept of *Pao* as a Basis for Social Relations in China" in *Chinese Thoughts and Institutions*, ed. John K. Fairbank, (Chicago, 1957), p. 291.
29. *LYCC*, XIII, 5420–21.
30. Ibid., XIII, 5426.
31. Ibid., XIII, 5440–41.
32. Liu Wu-chi, *An Introduction to Chinese Literature* (Bloomington, 1966), pp. 146–49, 220–24.
33. See *chüan* 7 of *Chin-ku ch'i-kuan* (*Modern and Ancient Strange Stories*) (Hong Kong, 1966), pp. 62–84. See also *The Courtesan's Jewel Box*, trans. Yang Hsien-yi and Gladys Yang (Peking: 1957).
34. *LYCC*, XIII, 5465–67.
35. Ibid., XIII, 5505–6.
36. Ibid., XIII, 5575.
37. Quoted in Huang Li-chen, p. 216.
38. *LYCC*, XIII, 5628–29.
39. Ibid., XIII, 5698.
40. Ibid., XIII, 5700–701.
41. Ibid., XIII, 5691–92.
42. Ibid., XIII, 5712–13.
43. Ibid., XIII, 5716.
44. Ibid.
45. William Shakespeare, *King Lear*, ed. George Lyman Kittredge, (Waltham, Mass., 1967), p. 5.
46. See *The Complete Works of Geoffrey Chaucer*, 2nd ed., ed. F. N. Robinson (Boston, 1957), pp. 101–14.

Chapter Three

1. *Shih-erh lou* is a collection of twelve short stories and the title of each is named after a *lou*, a word almost impossible to render in English because of its diversity of meanings. It could mean a two-story house, a chamber, an upper story, or a tower. For consistency, we have chosen the word "tower," though it might not be appropriate in every instance.

The twelve *lous* are the following: (1) *Ho-ying lou;* (2) *Tuo-chin lou;* (3) *San-yü lou;* (4) *Hsia-yi lou;* (5) *Kuei-cheng lou;* (6) *Ts'ui-ya lou;* (7) *Fu-yün lou;* (8) *Shih-chin lou;* (9) *Ho-kuei lou;* (10) *Feng-hsien lou;* (11) *Sheng-wo lou;* and (12) *Wen-kuo lou*. For equivalents in English, see the text; see also *Li Yü's Twelve Towers*, retold by Nathan Mao, p. vii, who translated the titles as follows: (1) "The Reflections in the Water"; (2) "The Jackpot"; (3) "Buried Treasure"; (4) "The Magic Mirror"; (5) "The Swindler"; (6) "The Elegant Eunuch"; (7) "The Crafty Maid"; (8) "Marital Frustrations"; (9)

"The Stoic Lover"; (10) "The Male Heir"; (11) "Father and Son"; and (12) "The Hermit."

For an explanation of its other title, *Chüeh-shih ming-yen*, and the relationship between *Shih-erh lou* and *Wu-sheng hsi*, see Liu Ts'un-yan, *Chinese Popular Fiction in Two London Libraries* (Hong Kong, 1968), pp. 112–16.

2. *LYCC*, XIV, 5846. See also *Li Yü's Twelve Towers*, p. 7; hereafter cited as *TW*.

3. *LYCC*, XIV, 5862–63; *TW*, 10–11.

4. *LYCC*, XIV, 5863–64; *TW*, 11.

5. *LYCC*, XIV, 5869–70; *TW*, 12.

6. *LYCC*, XIV, 5885–86; *TW*, 13.

7. *LYCC*, XIV, 5886–87; *TW*, 13.

8. *LYCC*, XIV, 5923; *TW*, 20.

9. *LYCC*, XIV, 5957–58; *TW*, 24–25.

10. *LYCC*, III, 1169–70; see also II, 945–46.

11. Ibid., XIV, 5959; see also Huang Li-chen, p. 184.

12. *LYCC*, XIV, 6037–39; *TW*, 34–35.

13. Jack Matthews, ed., *Archetypal Themes in the Modern Story* (New York, 1973), pp. 233–34.

14. *LYCC*, XIV, 6057–58; *TW*, 38.

15. *LYCC*, XIV, 6061; *TW*, 38–39. Sun P'in and P'ang Chüan were two famous political and military strategists who lived during the Warring Kingdoms period. Meng Pen and Hsia Yü are two ancient heroes recorded in the classics. Su Ch'in and Chang Yi were statesmen and sophists during the Warring Kingdoms period; for Sun P'in and P'ang Chüan, see *Shih-chi, chüan* 65; Su Ch'in and Chang Yi, *chüan* 69–70.

16. *LYCC*, XIV, 6062; *TW*, 39.

17. *LYCC*, XIV, 6113–16; *TW*, 48.

18. See Shizue Matsuda, "The Beauty and the Scholar in Li Yü's Short Stories," *Studies in Short Fiction* 9, no. 3 (Summer, 1973), 276.

19. *LYCC*, XV, 6320; *TW*, 83.

20. Sun K'ai-ti, "Li Li-weng yü *Shih-erh lou*," p. 430.

21. Robert F. Davidson, ed., *The Search for Meaning in Life* (New York, 1962), p. 92.

22. *LYCC*, XV, 6394.

23. Davidson, p. 94.

24. *LYCC*, XV, 6426–27; *TW*, 102.

25. *LYCC*, XV, 6427–28; *TW*, 102.

26. Quoted in Joanna F. Handlin, "Lü K'un's New Audience: The Influence of Women's Literacy on Sixteenth Century Thought," in *Women in Chinese Society*, ed. M. Wolf and Roxane Witke (Stanford, 1975), p. 14.

27. Roxane Witke, "Mao Tse-tung, Women and Suicide," in *Women in China*, ed. Marilyn B. Young (Ann Arbor, 1973), p. 13.

28. *LYCC*, XV, 6452–53.
29. Kenneth Latourette, *The Chinese, Their History and Culture*, 4th ed., (New York, 1971), pp. 568–69.
30. *LYCC*, XV, 6489; *TW*, 113.
31. *LYCC*, XV, 6495; *TW*, 114.
32. *LYCC*, XV, 6537–38.
33. Quoted in Shih Chung-wen, *The Golden Age of Chinese Drama: Yüan Tsa-chü* (Princeton, 1976), p. 97.
34. Quoted in Wing-tsit Chan, "The Story of Chinese Philosophy," in *The Chinese Mind*, ed. Charles Moore (Honolulu, 1974), p. 35.
35. Sun K'ai-ti, "Li Li-weng yü *Shih-erh lou*," p. 435.

Chapter Four

1. See "The San-yen: Narrative Style," in *The Colloquial Short Story in China*, pp. 29–46; W. W. Idema, "Storytelling and the Short Story in China," in *Chinese Vernacular Fiction* (Leiden, 1974), pp. 4–12.
2. *LYCC*, XIV, 6133.
3. Ibid., XV, 6200–201; *TW*, 63–64.
4. *LYCC*, XV, 6351; *TW*, 89.
5. *LYCC*, XV, 6352; *TW*, 89.
6. *LYCC*, XV, 6534; *TW*, 121.
7. *LYCC*, XIII, 5590–91.
8. Ibid., XII, 5235.
9. Ibid., XII, 5086–87.
10. Ibid., XIV, 5889; *TW*, 14.
11. *LYCC*, XV, 6212–14; *TW*, 66; see also *LYCC*, V, 2221.
12. Ibid., XIV, 6193–94; *TW*, 62.
13. *LYCC*, XV, 6051–52; *TW*, 37.
14. Two daughters of the legendary Emperor Yao in ancient records. See David Hawkes, *Ch'u Tz'u* (Oxford, 1959), p. 37.
15. *LYCC*, XV, 6208–9; *TW*, 65.
16. *LYCC*, XIV, 6133–34; *TW*, 52.
17. For information on the peach-blossom fountain, see H. A. Giles, *Gems of Chinese Literature* (Taipei, n.d.), p. 104.
18. *LYCC*, XV, 6537–38; *TW*, 122.
19. *LYCC*, XV, 6347–48; *TW*, 88.
20. E. M. Forster, *Aspects of the Novel* (London, 1966), pp. 75–77.
21. John L. Bishop, "Some Limitations of Chinese Fiction," in *Studies in Chinese Literature*, p. 245.
22. Shih Chung-wen, pp. 47–48.
23. Northrop Frye, *Anatomy of Criticism* (Princeton, 1973), p. 304.
24. Ibid., p. 305.
25. Shih Chung-wen, p. 71.
26. See H. C. Chang, *Chinese Literature* (Edinburgh, 1973), p. 12.

Chapter Five

1. Helmut Martin, ed., *Wu-sheng hsi* (Taipei, 1969), pp. 8–9; see Sun, "Li Li-weng yü *Shih-erh lou*," pp. 415–16. Sun suspects that this work could have been edited by another scholar based on Li Yü's original manuscript, but the quality of the work is not very high.

2. *Li Li-weng über Das Theater*, pp. 279–301.

3. *Jou Pu Tuan (Prayer Mat of Flesh)* trans. Richard Martin from Franz Kuhn's German version (New York, 1963), pp. 358–76; hereafter cited as Martin.

4. James Hightower, "Franz Kuhn and His Translation of *Jou P'u T'uan*," *Oriens Extremus* 8 (1961), 256.

5. Jeremey Ingalls, "Mr. Ch'ing-yin and the Chinese Erotic Novel," *Yearbook of Comparative Literature*, no. 13 (1964), 60. "Mr. Ch'ing-yin" is the pseudonym adopted by the author of *Jou p'u-t'uan*.

6. Quoted in Hightower, "Franz Kuhn . . . ," p. 255; Sun, "Li Li-weng yü *Shih-erh lou*," p. 381. For the original text, see *Tsai-yüan tsa-chih*, *chüan* 1 in *Liao-hai ts'ung-shu*, series 4.

7. Lu Hsün, *A Brief History of Chinese Fiction*, trans. Yang Hsien-yi and Gladys Yang (Connecticut, 1973), p. 239.

8. Sun K'ai-ti, *Chung-kuo t'ung-su hsiao-shuo mu-lu (Bibliography of Chinese Popular Fiction)*, rev. ed. (Peking, 1957), p. 156; also quoted in Hightower, p. 255.

9. *Li Li-weng über Das Theater*, pp. 279–301; *LYCC*, I, 3, 5 ("Pien-yen" [Introduction]).

10. R. H. Van Gulik, *Sexual Life in Ancient China*, pp. 301–6.

11. Ibid., pp. 264–65.

12. Ch'ing-yin hsien-sheng, *Jou p'u-t'uan* (Kuei-yu edition of 1633) ch. 3, p. 4b; ch. 7, pp. 8b–9a. Since specific story titles are given in the text, only page numbers in *Jou p'u-t'uan* will be given; hereafter cited as *JPT*.

13. *JPT*, ch. 2, p. 1b; ch. 4, p. 3a.

14. Ibid., ch. 12, p. 6a.

15. *LYCC*, XV, 6423–24.

16. *JPT*, ch. 19, p. 2a.

17. Ibid., ch. 3, p. 4b.

18. Ibid., ch. 2, p. 3a.

19. Ibid., ch. 15, p. 14b.

20. Ibid., ch. 2, p. 7a.

21. *LYCC*, XV, 6213.

22. *JPT*, ch. 5, p. 3b.

23. *LYCC*, XIII, 5397.

24. *JPT*, ch. 7, p. 2b.

25. *Li Li-weng über Das Theater*, p. 298.

26. Van Gulik, p. xii.

27. Van Gulik's book deals with this subject exclusively.
28. C. T. Hsia, *The Classic Chinese Novel* (New York, 1968), pp. 167–68.
29. Van Gulik, pp. 123–24.
30. Martin, pp. 366–67.
31. C. T. Hsia, "Review of *Jou Pu Tuan*," *Journal of Asian Studies* 12, no. 2 (February, 1964), 298–301.
32. Ibid., p. 299.
33. *JPT*, ch. 6, pp. 7a–7b; Martin, p. 83. We have consulted Martin's English translation throughout this chapter and have made changes to more accurately reflect the original text.
34. *JPT*, ch. 8, p. 8b.
35. Ibid., ch. 17, pp. 1b–2a.
36. Ibid., ch. 4, p. 3a.
37. Ibid., ch. 15, p. 7a; Martin, pp. 230–31.
38. *JPT*, ch. 2, p. 6b; Martin, pp. 11–12.
39. *JPT*, ch. 3, p. 7b.
40. Ibid., ch. 6, pp. 1b–2a; Martin, p. 74.
41. *JPT*, ch. 10, pp. 4b–5a.
42. Ibid., ch. 16, p. 8b.
43. Ibid., ch. 12, p. 4a.
44. Ibid., ch. 14, p. 4b.
45. Ibid., ch. 8, p. 9a.
46. Ibid., ch. 17, pp. 14b–15a; Martin, pp. 281–82.
47. *JPT*, ch. 17, p. 15a; Martin, p. 282.
48. Martin, p. 282.
49. *JPT*, ch. 2, p. 11b.
50. Martin, p. 147.
51. *JPT*, ch. 7, p. 4b; Martin, pp. 95–96.
52. R. W. B. Lewis, *The American Adam* (Chicago, 1955), p. 153.
53. See Peter L. Thorsleve, Jr., *The Byronic Hero* (Minneapolis, 1965), p. 8.
54. *The Classic Chinese Novel*, p. 200.
55. *LYCC*, XIV, 6053–54; *TW*, 37.

Chapter Six

1. Masaru, Aoki, trans. Wang Ku-lu, *Chung-kuo chin-shih hsi-ch'ü shih* (Peking, 1958), I, 1.
2. Liu, *An Introduction to Chinese Literature*, p. 159. See also Chang Heng's (62–139 A.D.) "Hsi-ching *fu*" (A *fu* on the Western Capital) in the *Wen-hsüan* (compiled during the sixth century) (Hong Kong, 1960), I, 42–44.
3. *An Introduction to Chinese Literature*, p. 165.
4. Ibid., p. 166.

5. In his unpublished paper, "Mongol Influence on the Development of Northern Drama," Stephen West argues that even though the Mongols were influential in making drama flourish, they were not responsible for the rise of drama. Instead, West suggests that Chinese drama has existed at least since the eleventh century. To support his thesis related to drama's earlier origins, West cites four recent archeological finds in China: "Three have brought to light tomb tiles or frescoes that have pictorial representations of *yüan-pen* or *pei-ch'ü* acting troupes, and one has produced a miniature stage and five dolls that are replicas of a *yüan-pen* troupe. The earliest dated find is a group of three tiles from a Northern Sung tomb, unearthed in Honan in 1958. They show the role types of a Northern Sung *tsa-chü* engaged in performance. . . . This find has been particularly significant because the costumed characters show that a relatively complex drama was in process some one-hundred years before the development of either *hsi-wen* (Southern Sung drama) or *pei-ch'ü*. Significantly, when these finds are compared to another set of engravings of an acting troupe found on a sarcophagus in a tomb dated 1260, well into the flourishing period of *tsa-chü*, we find no distinct differences in either costuming or posturing. . . . The similarities between the characters of the engravings and the tomb tiles suggest a continuity in the impersonation of characters on stage, and provide strong evidence that drama, in the basic meaning of the word, existed long before the Yüan" (pp. 31–32).

6. *An Introduction to Chinese Literature*, pp. 170–71. For a special study of the structure of Yüan drama, see the following works by James I. Crump: "The Conventions and Craft of Yüan Drama," *Journal of the American Oriental Society* 91, no. 1 (January–March, 1971), 14–29; "The Elements of Yüan Drama," *Journal of Asian Studies* 17, no. 3 (May, 1958), 417–34; and "Yüan-pen, Yüan Drama's Rowdy Ancestor," *Literature East and West* 14, no. 4 (1970), 473–90.

7. *An Introduction to Chinese Literature*, pp. 253–57. For a discussion of T'ang Hsien-tsu, see C. T. Hsia's "Time and the Human Condition in the Plays of T'ang Hsien-tsu," in *Self and Society in Ming Thought*, ed. William T. de Bary (New York, 1970), pp. 249–90.

8. Man Sai-cheong, "A Study of Li Yü on Drama" (M.A. thesis, University of Hong Kong, 1970), pp. 1–2; hereafter cited as Man.

9. Man, p. 5. See also Wang Li, *Han-yü yin-yün hsüeh* (Shanghai, 1957), pp. 488–505.

10. Man, pp. 1–33. See also Aoki, *Chung-kuo chin-shih hsi-ch'ü shih*, vol. II, appendix 3, compiled by Wang Ku-lu, the translator.

11. For details of Li's own illustrations, see *LYCC*, V, 2184–94.

12. Arthur Waley, *The Secret History of the Mongols* (London, 1963), p. 92.

13. *Ibid.*, p. 93.

14. *LYCC*, V, 1927–30.
15. Ibid., V, 1973.
16. Ibid., V, 2051–52.
17. Ibid., V, 1980.
18. *LYCC*, V, 1977.
19. Ibid.
20. Ibid., V, 1933–34.
21. Waley, *The Secret History of the Mongols*, p. 89.
22. *LYCC*, V, 1984. See also Man, p. 51.
23. Carl E. Bain, ed., *Drama* (New York: 1973), p. xiii.
24. *LYCC*, V, 1951.
25. Ibid., V, 1960.
26. Ibid., V, 1962.
27. Ibid., V, 1960–61; Man, pp. 65–66.
28. *LYCC*, V, 1964–65.
29. Ibid., V, 1940.
30. *An Introduction to Chinese Literature*, p. 259.
31. *LYCC*, V, 1957–58; Man, p. 89.
32. *LYCC*, V, 1947; Man, pp. 90–91.
33. *LYCC*, V, 1947–48.
34. Ibid., V, 1953.
35. Ibid., V, 1952.
36. Ibid.
37. Ibid., V, 1937.
38. Quoted in *Dramatic Theory and Criticism*, ed. Bernard F. Dukore (New York, 1974), p. 807.
39. Ibid., p. 811.
40. *LYCC*, V, 2079.
41. *LYCC*, V, 2084.
42. Ibid., V, 2085–86.
43. Ibid., V, 2087.
44. Ibid.
45. Ibid., V, 2088.
46. Ibid., V, 2051.
47. Ibid., V, 1969.
48. Ibid.; Man, pp. 43–44.
49. *LYCC*, V, 1983.
50. Ibid., V, 1969–70; Man, pp. 44–45.
51. Quoted in *Dramatic Theory and Criticism*, p. 70.
52. *LYCC*, V, 1975; Man, pp. 48–49.
53. *An Introduction to Chinese Literature*, p. 170.
54. Chu Tung-jun, "Li Yü hsi-chü-lun tsung-shu," quoted in *LYCC*, XV, 6708.

55. *LYCC*, XV, 6709. See also Tsang, *Yüan-ch'ü hsüan*, vol. 1, *Ssu-pu pei-yao* ed. p. 1a.
56. *LYCC*, V, 2043–44; Man, pp. 115–16.
57. *LYCC*, V, 2044.
58. Ibid., V, 2052–53.
59. Ibid., V, 2045; Man, p. 121.
60. *LYCC*, V, 2046–68.
61. Ibid., V, 2052–53; see also Man, p. 122.
62. *LYCC*, V, 2072.
63. Ibid., V, 2070–71; Man, p. 75.
64. *LYCC*, V, 2093.
65. Ibid., V, 2095–96.
66. Ibid., V, 2100.
67. *LYCC*, V, 2103.
68. Ibid., V, 2103–4.
69. Ibid., V, 2109–11.
70. Ibid., V, 2168–69; Man, pp. 157–58.
71. *LYCC*, V, 2167–68.
72. *LYCC*, V, 2190–94.
73. Ibid., V, 2095; Man, pp. 139–40.
74. *LYCC*, V, 2157–58.
75. Ibid., V, 2159; Man, p. 146.
76. *LYCC*, V, 2164.
77. *LYCC*, V, 2165.
78. Ibid., V, 2158; Man, p. 145.
79. *LYCC*, V, 2172–73; Man, pp. 150–51.
80. *LYCC*, V, 2175–77; Man, pp. 151–52.
81. *LYCC*, V, 2183; Man, p. 153.
82. *LYCC*, V, 2182.
83. *LYCC*, V, 2062.
84. Ibid., V, 2058.
85. James J. Y. Liu, *Chinese Theories of Literature* (Chicago, 1975), p. 92.
86. Man, p. 173.

Chapter Seven

1. Quoted in Sun K'ai-ti, "Li Li-weng yü *Shih-erh lou*," p. 400. This work of Tung's, also titled *Ch'un-hsiang chui-pi*, is included in the *Ts'ung-shu Shuo-ling*.
2. Sun, p. 380. See also *chüan* 246 of *Ts'ung-shu Shuo-ling*.
3. Sun, p. 381. See also *chüan* 1 of *Ts'ung-shu Shuo-ling*.
4. Sun, pp. 381–82. See also *chüan* 5 of *Ts'ung-shu Shuo-ling*.
5. Lu Hsün, *A Brief History of Chinese Fiction*, pp. 110, 239.

6. Liu Ta-chieh, *Chung-kuo wen-hsüeh fa-chan-shih* (Hong Kong, 1961), *chüan hsia*, pp. 305–6.

7. Cheng Chen-to, *Ch'a-t'u-pen Chung-kuo wen-hsüeh-shih* (Peking, 1959), II, 1019–23.

8. Chou Tso-jen, *K'u-chu tsa-chi*, 2nd ed. (Shanghai, 1941), pp. 81–86.

9. *An Introduction to Chinese Literature*, pp. 257–59.

10. Martin, p. 369.

Appendix One

1. For a detailed study of *Wu-sheng hsi* versus *Lien-ch'eng pi*, see Sun K'ai-ti, "Li Li-weng chu *Wu-sheng hsi* chi *Lien-ch'eng pi* chieh-t'i," *Bulletin of the National Library of Peiping (Kuo-li Pei-p'ing t'u-shu-kuan kuan-k'an)* 6, no. 1 (January–February, 1932), 9–25; *LYCC*, XV, 6599–614.

2. *Wu-sheng hsi*, ed. Helmut Martin (Taipei, 1969), pp. 9–11.

Appendix Two

1. L. Carrington Goodrich, *The Literary Inquisition of Ch'ien-lung* (New York, 1966), p. 6.

2. *LYCC*, I, 29–31.

3. Ibid., I, 19–21.

4. Sun K'ai-ti, "Li Li-weng yü *Shih-erh lou*," p. 403.

5. Ibid., p. 402.

6. Ibid., p. 410.

7. Ibid., p. 413.

8. Huang Li-chen, p. 146.

9. *An Introduction to Chinese Literature*, p. 258.

Selected Bibliography

PRIMARY SOURCES

Li Yü ch'üan-chi (*Complete Works of Li Yü*). Edited by Helmut Martin. 15 vols. Taipei: Ch'eng-wen ch'u-pan-she), 1970. It includes the complete *Yi-chia yen, Hsien-ch'ing ou-chi, Wu-sheng hsi, Shih-erh lou,* and ten dramatic plays. Also included are critical essays by Sun K'ai-ti, Hu Meng-hua, and Chu Tung-jun. A useful anthology for scholars interested in Li Yü, even though the printing of some of the original woodblock editions is poor and many passages are illegible.

Li-weng ch'ü-hua. Taipei: Kuang-wen shu-chü, 1970. Includes Li's dramatic theory as originally printed in *Hsien-ch'ing ou-chi.*

Wu-sheng hsi. Edited by Helmut Martin. Taipei: Ku-t'ing shu-wu, 1969. A limited edition of the original manuscript preserved at the Sonkeikaku Library in Japan. Printing is of low quality.

Shih-erh lou. A popular, undated edition printed in Hong Kong by the Kuang-chih Book Co. It remains the most inexpensive and readily available edition.

Jou p'u-t'uan.
   1. The *Kuei-yu* woodblock edition of 1633. (Kuhn miscalculated this cyclic year to be 1634 in his Note to the German translation of this work.)
   2. *Tsui-yüeh Hsüan* (Studio) woodblock edition, undated. A copy is kept in the collection of the Peking Library.
   3. Japanese edition of 1705. (A photolithographical edition reprinted from the *Tsui-yüeh Hsüan* woodblock edition is available.)
   4. Japanese edition of the Meiji period (1868–1912), date uncertain.
   5. Chinese lithographic edition of 1869 (the cyclic being *chi-ssu,* the eighth year of T'ung-chih. Sun K'ai-ti made a mistake in his bibliography by calling it a Kuang-hsü edition.)
   6. Chinese reprint of 1943.

SECONDARY SOURCES

AOKI, MASARU. *Chung-kuo chin-shih hsi-ch'ü-shih* (*History of Chinese Drama in the Recent Centuries*). Translated into Chinese by Wang

Ku-lu. Peking: Tso-chia ch'u-pan-she, 1958. Remains one of the defini-
tive studies of Chinese drama.
BISHOP, JOHN L. *The Colloquial Short Story in China: A Study of the
San-Yen Collections*. Cambridge: Harvard University Press, 1956. A
major study of the development of the Chinese short story.
————. "Some Limitations of Chinese Fiction." In *Studies in Chinese Lit-
erature*, edited by John L. Bishop, pp. 237–45. Cambridge: Harvard
University Press, 1966. Notes some differences between Chinese and
Western fiction.
CHAN, WING-TSIT. "The Story of Chinese Philosophy." In *The Chinese
Mind*, edited by Charles A. Moore, pp. 31–76. Honolulu: The Univer-
sity of Hawaii Press, 1967. Discusses the major schools of Chinese
philosophy.
CHANG, H. C. *Chinese Literature*. Edinburgh: Edinburgh University
Press, 1973. A study and anthology of Chinese fiction in the colloquial
language and drama.
*Chekiang Hsin-ch'eng hsien-chih (Gazeteer of the District of Hsin-ch'eng,
Chekiang)* (1679). *Chüan* 15, p. 10b. A brief account of Li Yü's life.
CH'EN, TIEH-I. "Ch'ing-t'ai ti hsi-ch'ü shih-chien-chia Li Li-weng" ("Li
Li-weng, a Ch'ing Dynasty Drama Practitioner"). *Wen-hsüeh shih-
chieh (Literature World)*, no. 46 (1965), 63–66, 86. Useful for general
reference.
CH'EN, WAN-NAI. *Yüan Ming Ch'ing hsi-ch'ü shih (A History of Yüan,
Ming, and Ch'ing Drama)*. Taipei: Commercial Press, 1966. A good
reference book.
CHENG, CHEN-TO. *Ch'a-t'u pen Chung-kuo wen-hsüeh shih (An Illustrated
History of Chinese Literature)*. Peking: Wen-hsüeh ku-chi k'an-hsing-
she, 1959. One of the best histories of Chinese literature.
————. *Chung-kuo wen-hsüeh yen-chiu (Studies in Chinese Literature)*.
Peking: Tso-chia ch'u-pan-she, 1957. Contains several essays on Yüan
drama.
CHIANG, JUI-TSAO. *Hsiao-shuo k'ao-cheng (A Textual Study of Fiction)*.
Shanghai: Commercial Press, 1957. A most useful reference book.
CHOU, I-PAI. *Chung-kuo hsi-ch'ü shih chiang-tso (Lectures on the History
of Chinese Drama)*. Peking: Chung-kuo hsi-chü ch'u-pan-she, 1958.
Informative.
CHOU, TSO-JEN. "Li Li-weng yü Chien-hao fa-shih" ("Li Li-weng and Priest
Chien-hao"). *Yü-ssu (Language Threads)*, no. 5 (December, 1924).
Early study of Li Yü, but the essay is too brief and without depth.
CHU, HSIANG. "P'i-p'ing-chia Li Li-weng" ("The Critic Li Li-weng"). *Yü-
ssu*, no. 19 (March, 1925). Discusses Li's role as a critic.
CHU, TUNG-JUN. "Li Yü hsi-ch'ü-lun ts'ung-shu" ("A Discussion on Li Yü's
Dramatic Theory"). *Quarterly Journal of Liberal Arts* (Wu-han Univer-
sity) 3 (1934), 729–752. Evaluates Li Yü's contributions to the de-
velopment of Chinese drama.

CH'Ü, T'UNG-TSU. *Law and Society in Ancient China.* Paris: Mouton, 1961. One of the best on the subject.
CRUMP, JAMES I. "The Conventions and Craft of Yüan Drama." *Journal of the American Oriental Society* 91, no. 1 (January–March, 1971), 14–29. Informative.
————. "The Elements of Yüan Opera." *Journal of Asian Studies* 17, no. 3 (May, 1958), 417–34. Important to the study of Yüan drama.
EDWARDS, E. D. *Chinese Prose Literature of the T'ang Period.* London: Probsthain, 1938. A major work of scholarship on T'ang prose literature.
GOODRICH, L. CARRINGTON. *The Literary Inquisition of Ch'ien-lung.* New York: Paragon Book Reprint Co., 1966. Discusses the history of Chinese censorship.
HANAN, PATRICK. *The Chinese Short Story.* Cambridge: Harvard University Press, 1973. Discusses dating, authorship, and the composition of Chinese fiction.
Hang-chou fu-chih (Gazetteer of the Prefecture of Hang-chou) 1922). *Chüan* 170, p. 1b. Some biographical information on Li Yü.
HIGHTOWER, JAMES. "Franz Kuhn and His Translation of *Jou P'u T'uan.*" *Oriens Extremus* 8 (1961), 252–57. Questions Li Yü's authorship of the *Prayer Mat of Flesh.* Arguments not convincing.
HSIA, C. T. *The Classic Chinese Novel: A Critical Introduction.* New York: Columbia University Press, 1968. A brilliant analysis of six major Chinese novels.
————. "Review of Kuhn's Translation of *Jou P'u T'uan.*" *Journal of Asian Studies* 22, no. 2 (February, 1964), 298–301. Discusses the literary qualities of the *Prayer Mat of Flesh.*
HSÜ, HAN-CHANG. "Li Li-weng nien-p'u" ("A Chronological Biography of Li Li-weng"). *Nan-feng (The South Wind)* 10, no. 1 (June, 1934). Sketchy.
HU, MENG-HUA. "Wen-hsüeh p'i-p'ing-chia Li Li-weng" ("The Literary Critic Li Li-weng"). In *Li Yü ch'üan-chi (Complete Works of Li Yü),* edited by Helmut Martin, XV, 6681–95. Taipei, 1973. Discusses Li's dramatic theory.
HUANG, LI-CHEN. *Li Yü yen-chiu (A Study of Li Yü).* Taipei: Chun-wen hsüeh ch'u-pan-she, 1974. A good biographical treatment, but weak on critical analysis of Li's works.
IDEMA, W. L. *Chinese Vernacular Fiction.* Leiden: E. J. Brill, 1974. A valuable study.
INGALLS, JEREMEY. "Mr. Ch'ing-yin and the Chinese Erotic Novel." *Yearbook of Comparative Literature,* no. 13 (1964), 60–63. Suggests that the author of the *Prayer Mat of Flesh* might have been a woman.
KLOSSOWSKI, PIERRE. *Jeou P'ou T'ouan.* Paris: Editions Jean-Jacques Pauvet, 1962. A French translation of the *Prayer Mat of Flesh.*
KU, TUN-JOU. "Li Li-weng nien-p'u" ("A Chronological Biography of Li Li-weng") in *Harvard Yen-ching hsüeh-she lun-wen chi (Harvard-*

Yen-ching Collection of Academic Articles). No date. Cited in Helmut Martin's *Li Li-weng über Das Theater* (Heidelberg, 1966), p. 322.

————. "Li Li-weng p'eng-pei k'ao-ch'uan" ("A Study of Li Li-weng's Friends"). *Chih-chiang hsüeh-pao* (*Chih-chiang Academic Journal*), no. 4 (August, 1935). Informative.

————. "Li Li-weng tz'u-hsüeh ch'ien-shuo" ("An Introductory Discussion of Li Li-weng on *tz'u*"). *Chung-hua hsüeh-shu-yüan Chung-kuo wen-hsüeh hui-k'an* (*Journal of the Chinese Literary Association of Chinese Academic College*) (Taipei) (1967), 21–35. A judicious study of Li's *tz'u* poetry.

————. "*Plays Without Sound*, A Collection of Short Stories by Li Li-weng (1611–1680)." *Books and Writers* (Taipei) 5 (March, 1969), 761–66. Discusses Li's use of the vernacular in Li's collection, *Drama Without Sound*.

Kuang-hsü Lan-ch'i hsien-chih (*The Kuang-hsü Gazetteer of the District of Lan-ch'i*). (1888). *Chüan* 5, p. 41a; *chüan* 8, p. 59a. One of the most detailed biographies of Li Yü.

KUHN, FRANZ, trans. *Jou Pu Tuan* (*The Prayer Mat of Flesh*). Zurich: Verlag die Waage, 1959; Translated by Richard Martin into English from the German version of Kuhn. New York: Grove Press, 1966. Readable and inexpensive.

K'UNG, LING-CHING, Comp. *Chung-kuo hsiao-shuo shih-liao* (*Source Materials on Chinese Fiction*). Shanghai: Ku-tien-wen-hsüeh ch'u-pan-she, 1957. A useful reference book.

KUO, SHAO-YÜ. *Chung-kuo wen-hsüeh p'i-p'ing shih* (*A History of Chinese Literary Criticism*). Shanghai: Commercial Press, 1961. A standard comprehensive treatment of Chinese literary criticism.

LAI, MING. *A History of Chinese Literature*. New York: Capricorn Books, 1964. A concise history of Chinese literature.

LI, MAN-KUEI. "Li Yü." In *Eminent Chinese of the Ch'ing Period*, edited by Arthur W. Hummel, I, 495–97. Washington, D.C.: U.S. Government Printing Office, 1943–1944. A good summary of Li Yü's life, even though it erroneously gives Li's place of birth as Ju-kao, Kiangsu.

LIN, YUTANG. *My Country and My People*. New York: The John Day Co., 1935. Contains translations from Li Yü's *A Temporary Lodge of My Leisure Thoughts*.

————. "On Charm in Women." *China Critic* 12, no. 11 (March, 1936) 231–33. An interesting piece of translation from Li's *A Temporary Lodge*.

————. *The Importance of Living*. New York: The John Day Co., 1940. Contains translations from Li's *A Temporary Lodge of My Leisure Thoughts*.

————. *The Importance of Understanding*. Cleveland: The World Publishing Co., 1960. Contains translations from Li's *A Temporary Lodge of My Leisure Thoughts*.

LIU, JAMES, J. Y. *Chinese Theories of Literature.* Chicago: University of Chicago Press, 1975. The best coverage of the subject in English.

LIU, TA-CHIEH. *Chung-kuo wen-hsüeh fa-chan shih (A History of the Flourishing of Chinese Literature).* Taipei: Taiwan Chung-hua Book Co., 1967. Still one of the best and most comprehensive histories of Chinese literature.

LIU, TS'UN-YAN. *Buddhist and Taoist Influences on Chinese Novels.* Wiesbaden: Otto Harrassowitz, 1962. Definitive and exhaustive on the subject.

————. *Chinese Popular Fiction in Two London Libraries.* Hong Kong: Lungmen Book Co., 1967. Provides useful bibliographical information.

————. *Selected Papers from the Hall of Harmonious Wind.* Leiden: E. J. Brill, 1976. A collection of Professor Liu's papers on Chinese literature. Useful reference.

LIU, WU-CHI. *An Introduction to Chinese Literature.* Bloomington: Indiana University Press, 1966. Still one of the best introductions to Chinese literature.

LU HSÜN. *A Brief History of Chinese Fiction.* Translated by Yang Hsien-yi and Gladys Yang. Reprint. Connecticut: Hyperion Press, 1973. Still sound and useful.

MAN, SAI-CHEONG. "A Study of Li Yü on Drama." M.A. thesis, University of Hong Kong, 1970. Very useful.

————, trans. "Li Yü on the Performing Arts," *Renditions,* no. 3 (Autumn, 1974), 62–65. Good for general reference.

MAO, NATHAN K., trans. *Li Yü's Twelve Towers.* Hong Kong: The Chinese University of Hong Kong, 1975. A free translation.

————, trans. "Tower of the Returning Crane." *Renditions,* no. 1 (Autumn, 1973), 25–35. A free translation.

————. "The Tradition of Seduction in Chinese Literature." *Enquiry* 1, no. 3 (Autumn, 1967), 1–11.

MARTIN, HELMUT. *Li Li-weng über Das Theater (Li Li-weng on the Theater).* Taipei: Mei Ya Publications, Inc., 1968. Excellent notes and bibliography. One of the most important studies on Li Yü.

MATSUDA, SHIZUE. "The Beauty and the Scholar in Li Yü's Short Stories." *Short Fiction* 10, no. 3 (Summer, 1973), 271–80. A very interesting discussion of the love theme in Li Yü's short stories.

MENG YAO. *Chung-kuo hsi-ch'ü shih (A History of Chinese Drama).* 4 vols. Taipei: Ch'uan-chi wen-hsüeh-she, 1965. Suitable for general reference.

————. *Chung-kuo hsiao-shuo shih (A History of Chinese Fiction).* 4 vols. Taipei: Wen-hsing shu-tien, 1966. Good for reference.

POZDNEEVA, L. D. "Zametki ob Epoche prosveshcheniia v Kitae" ("Notes on the Age of Enlightenment in China"). *Narody Azii i Afriki* 6 (1972). Useful for general reference.

PRŮŠEK, J. "Urban Centers: The Cradle of Popular Fiction." In *Studies in*

Chinese Literary Genres, edited by C. Birch, pp. 259–98. Berkeley: University of California Press, 1974. Readable and illuminating.

SHIH, CHUNG-WEN. *The Golden Age of Chinese Drama: Yüan Tsa-chü.* Princeton: Princeton University Press, 1976. Studies the conventions and themes of Yüan drama.

SUN K'AI-TI. *Chung-kuo t'ung-su hsiao-shuo shu-mu (A Catalogue of Chinese Works of Popular Fiction).* Rev. ed. Peking: Tso-chia ch'u-pan-she, 1957. An important reference book.

————. "Li Li-weng chu *Wu-sheng hsi* chi *Lien-ch'eng pi* chieh-ti" ("Li Li-weng's *Drama Without Sound* is *Lien-ch'eng pi:* An Explanation"). *Kuo-li Pei-p'ing t'u-shu-kuan kuan-k'an (National Pei-p'ing Library Journal)* 6, no. 1 (January–February, 1932), 9–25. A very important textual study of the *Drama Without Sound.*

————. "Li Li-weng yü *Shih-erh lou*" ("Li Li-weng and the *Twelve Towers*"). *Library Science Quarterly* (Peking) 9, nos. 3–4 (1935), 379–441. One of the earliest studies on Li Yü. Informative.

————. "*Wu-sheng hsi* shih-erh hui" ("The Twelve Chapters of *Drama Without Sound*"). In Sun's *Jih-pen Tung-ching so-chien Chung-kuo hsiao-shuo shu-mu (A Descriptive Catalogue of Chinese Works of Fiction Seen in Tokyo)*, pp. 23–26. Shanghai: Shang-tsa ch'u-pan-she, 1953. A very important textual study of the *Drama Without Sound.*

SZE, MAI-MAI. *The Way of Chinese Painting.* New York: Vintage Books, 1956. An inexpensive paperback. Contains selections from the *Painting Patterns of the Mustard Seed Garden.*

T'AN CHENG-PI. *Hua-pen yü ku-chü (Hua-pen and Old Drama).* Shanghai: Shanghai ku-tien-wen-hsüeh ch'u-pan-she, 1956. A very important general reference book.

VAN GULIK, R. H. *Sexual Life in Ancient China.* Leiden: E. J. Brill, 1961. Probably the best on the subject.

WALEY, ARTHUR. *Ballads and Stories from Tun-huang.* New York, Macmillan, 1963. Still useful.

————. *The Secret History of the Mongols.* London: Allen & Unwin 1963. Illuminating.

WANG, LI. *Han-yü yin-yün hsüeh (Chinese Phonology).* Peking: Chung-hua Book Co., 1956. A standard reference book on the subject.

WANG, TI-JAN. "P'i-p'ing-chia ti Li Li-weng" ("The Critic Li Li-weng"). *Mo-tun yüeh-k'an (Mo-tun Monthly)* 2, no. 5 (January, 1934). Discussion superficial.

WEST, STEPHEN. "Mongol Influence on the Development of Northern Drama." Paper prepared for the Yüan Conference, July, 1976, at York, Maine. West argues that the Mongols were not responsible for the rise of drama. Stimulating.

ZBIKOWSKI, T. *Early Nan-hsi Plays of the Southern Sung Period.* Warszawa, 1974. Important to the study of Chinese drama. A solid piece of scholarship.

Index

The listing of book and article titles in the index is not exhaustive. Authors and titles appearing solely as references in Notes and References and in Bibliography are not included.